The Karmapas and Their Mahāmudrā Forefathers

The Karmapas and Their Mahāmudrā Forefathers

AN ILLUSTRATED GUIDE

By Khenpo Sherap Phuntsok

Translated by Michele Martin

With images from the murals at Thrangu Tashi Yangtse Monastery

Painted by Lama Rigzin

Letters from
H. H. the Seventeenth Gyalwang Karmapa
and Khenchen Thrangu Rinpoche

Wisdom

Wisdom Publications
199 Elm Street
Somerville, MA 02144 USA
wisdompubs.org

Library of Congress Cataloging-in-Publication Data
Names: Shes-rab-phun-tshogs, Mkhan-po, author. | Rigzin, Lama, artist.
Title: The Karmapas and their Mahamudra forefathers : an illustrated guide / by Khenpo Sherap Phuntsok ; translated by Michele Martin.
Description: Somerville, MA : Wisdom Publications, 2016. | "With images from the murals at Thrangu Tashi Yangtse Monastery painted by Lama Rigzin." | Previously published: Kathmandu : Thrangu Tashi Choling Monastery, 2014. | Includes bibliographical references and index. | Translated from Tibetan. | Description based on print version record and CIP data provided by publisher; resource not viewed.
Identifiers: LCCN 2016019877 (print) | LCCN 2015041174 (ebook) | ISBN 9781614293040 (ebook) | ISBN 161429304X (ebook) | ISBN 9781614292807 | ISBN 9781614292807 q(paperback : alk paper) | ISBN 1614292809 q(paperback : alk paper) | ISBN 9781614293040 q(Ebook)
Subjects: LCSH: Bka'-brgyud-pa lamas—Tibet Region—Biography. | Bka'-brgyud-pa lamas—Tibet Region—Pictorial works. | BISAC: RELIGION / Buddhism / Tibetan. | RELIGION / Buddhism / Sacred Writings. | BIOGRAPHY & AUTOBIOGRAPHY / Religious.
Classification: LCC BQ7679.9.A2 (print) | LCC BQ7679.9.A2 S47 2016 (ebook) | DDC 294.3/9230922 [B] —dc23
LC record available at https://lccn.loc.gov/2016019877

ISBN 978-1-61429-280-7
Ebook ISBN 978-1-61429-304-0

20 19 18 17 16
5 4 3 2 1

The front cover depicts the Second Karmapa Karma Pakshi from the murals at Thrangu Tashi Yangtse painted by Lama Rigzin.
Cover and interior design by Gopa & Ted2, Inc.
Set in Diacritical Garamond Pro 11/15.4.

Wisdom Publications' books are printed on acid-free paper and meet the guidelines for permanence and durability of the Production Guidelines for Book Longevity of the Council on Library Resources.

This book was produced with environmental mindfulness. For more information, please visit wisdompubs.org/wisdom-environment.

Printed in the PRC.

Contents

THE KARMAPA

Excelling in the teachings of the Buddha with a mind steeped in virtue, Khenpo Sherap Phuntsok has carefully gathered the spiritual stories of the five Kagyü forefathers and the Karmapas. His book is based on authentic histories of the Dharma and was translated into English by Michele Martin. The stories were selected to illustrate the character of each master and the essential facts of his life, and are presented in a way that is not only accessible to the younger generation but will delight older students as well.

Further, so that the Karma Gardri style of painting and its rich tradition would not wane, in the main shrine room at Namo Buddha monastery, Lama Rigzin skillfully depicted the five forefathers and the sixteen Karmapas in a beautiful series of murals. Photographs of these murals, brilliant in color and of the highest quality, have been used to illustrate this book. In each of the portraits, the figures surrounding the central image—the yidam deities, teachers, and disciples—have been clearly identified.

I rejoice in this publication and pray that reading these spiritual biographies will inspire pure faith in the lineage and the wish to be skilled in benefiting oneself and others.

The Seventeenth Karmapa Ogyen Trinley Dorje
Dharamsala, Himachal Pradesh, India

VENERABLE THRANGU RINPOCHE

Generally, reading spiritual biographies inspires faith in the Buddha and his teachings, and in particular, the ones published here give rise to a devoted trust in the key instructions belonging to the practice lineage of the Karma Kamtsang. With this in mind, Khenpo Sherap Phuntsok has composed brief spiritual biographies of the masters Telopa and Naropa from India, of Marpa, Milarepa, and Gampopa, universally known in Tibet, and of the successive incarnations of the Gyalwang Karmapas to illustrate how they have benefited the teachings and living beings.

The thangka painter Rigzin together with artists connected to Thrangu Tashi Yangtse Monastery in Namo Buddha persevered through great difficulty to create these new images on the walls of its main shrine hall. Michele Martin translated the spiritual biographies, combined them with the paintings, and prepared the book for publication. I would like to express my thanks to everyone.

Khenchen Thrangu Rinpoche
Boudha, Nepal

A Note on Phonetics and Transliteration

The system of phonetics used by Wisdom Publications generally follows a Central Tibetan accent. The basis for transliteration is the Wylie version with a few minor changes. Only proper names and texts are capitalized, and the first letter, not the root letter, is capitalized. When the closing consonant at the end of a syllable matches the opening consonant of the next in the middle of a name, the extra consonant may be elided, as in Sengé (instead of Senggé). The names of contemporary Tibetans, or teachers who have traveled or published books in the West, are rendered as they do themselves, for example, the Sixteenth Karmapa Rigpe Dorje. The names that appear on the back of the paintings to identify the figures are given phonetically, and their transliterations can be found at the back in the List of Persons and Deities Featured in the Paintings. Sanskrit terms and all mantras are rendered as they appear in Sanskrit, e.g., ācārya, svāha, vajra, padma rather than atsarya, soha, benza, or pema.

Preface

Published together here for the first time are the concise life stories of the five Kagyü forefathers and the seventeen Karmapas, joined with their images portrayed in the new murals at Thrangu Tashi Yangtse Monastery in Nepal. This large complex of educational institutions, places of practice, and residences was founded by Kyabjé Yongzin Thrangu Rinpoche at the supreme place of Namo Buddha, or Takmo Lujin (Giving One's Body Generously to the Tigress). When the monastery was completed, the murals were painted on the extensive walls of the main shrine hall in a tradition known as Karma Gardri (the style of the Karmapas' encampment), a spacious way of painting prevalent at the Karmapas' residence. The images reproduced here depict the five Kagyü forefathers, the sixteen previous Karmapas, and the great protector of the teachings, Bernakchen.

Following the wishes of Thrangu Rinpoche, the painter Lama Rigzin worked wholeheartedly for many years, ignoring hardship and taking up difficulties with joy. To preserve the Karma Gardri tradition, Lama Rigzin created images in radiant color that are wonderfully detailed, precise, and subtle.

The life stories of the Karmapas were suggested by Thrangu Rinpoche, who knew that they are important for opening the door to the Buddhist teachings in general and particularly helpful to those who have met the precious teachings of the practice lineage known as the Karma Kamtsang. The key purpose of reading the life stories of the Gyalwang Karmapas as they continued to take rebirth over the centuries is to engender faith and devotion. Thrangu Rinpoche suggested that brief life stories written with the younger generation in mind would be very beneficial. Following his kind advice, in 2009 I wrote a book of short life stories of the Karmapas from the First through to the present Seventeenth Karmapa Ogyen Trinley Dorje. In 2013, at the request of the translator Michele Martin, I wrote the additional life stories of the five Kagyü forefathers.

The main sources for these five new spiritual biographies were Pawo Tsuklak Trengwa's *Origins of Dharma: A Feast for the Learned* and the life stories composed by Shamar Khachö Wangpo. The Karmapas' life stories were mainly taken from *The Golden Garland of the Kagyü* by Situ Chökyi Jungné, supplemented by Belo Tsewang Kunkhyap, and also from Pawo Rinpoché's *Origins of Dharma*. Since there is a one-year difference in the way years are calculated in Tibet and the West, the Tibetan tradition is followed here, since it stems from very reliable sources. The responsibility for the names of the figures below the images lies with the translator, who researched them for the English edition and also arranged for the photography of the murals. Lodrö Rabgye, who is from Malaysia and studied in the Vajra Vidya monastic college, kindly helped with designing and formatting the book. I rejoice immensely in the work of all those who have contributed to this project.

Khenpo Sherap Phuntsok
Namo Buddha, Nepal

About the Murals

The spiritual biographies presented here bring to life the lineage of the Gyalwang Karmapa, carrying the blessing of these great masters and their Kamtsang Kagyü traditions of practice and study. Lineage is also important to the artistic traditions of Tibet, though the history and styles of the numerous schools are still in the process of being defined and the artists' names are rare to find—a situation quite different from the Dharma lineages of practice and study whose masters' names have been carefully preserved. Yet there is much we can know from what is preserved in the oral traditions, texts, and the inscriptions on the paintings themselves.

Sources give different accounts of the history of the Karma Gardri (*Kar ma sgar bris*), the Encampment style of the Karmapas, and how it evolved. From the time of the Fourth to the Tenth, the Karmapas did not live in a fixed place but traveled throughout Tibet with tents, some for just one meditator and others big enough for a large shrine hall or the classrooms for its institutes of philosophical and tantric studies. The encampment was also home to many painters, including Tulku Namkha Tashi who is credited as the founder of the Karma Gardri style. He was a contemporary of the Eighth Karmapa (1507–54), holder of his Dharma lineage, and lama for the encampment. Considered to be an emanation as an artist, Tulku Namkha Tashi's fame spread throughout Tibet and beyond to China and Mongolia.

The Gardri style was based on the Menri (*Sman ris*) tradition, which originated in Central Tibet and embodied a spacious and natural approach, reflecting the influence of Chinese landscape painting. A famous example of this style is the Kagyü Sungenma (*Bka' brgyud zung rgan ma*), a set of thangkas depicting the Golden Garland of the Kagyü Masters. In the seventeenth century, two more artists with the name Tashi appeared: Chö Tashi, who developed the series of paintings known as the Golden Garland of the Kagyü, and also his contemporary, Karma Tashi. Along with Tulku Namkha Tashi, these artists are widely known as the Three Tashis, Experts in the Karma Gadri Style. Close to this time, Situ Panchen Chökyi Jungné (1700–1774), a great scholar and superb artist, began a new Karma Gardri style at his monastery of Palpung.

There are clear differences between the Gardri and Menri styles. In the former, the palette is more subdued and the landscape is sparse with a low horizon allowing for a spacious and, except for a yidam deity resting on stylized clouds, mostly empty sky. In the Menri style, the colors are brighter, the landscape has more detail, and the horizon sits near the top of the painting, giving more room to elaborate details in the landscape. At it happens, these differences in the palette and landscape also relate to the areas on the canvas where a painter has some leeway. Traditionally, when copying a set of images like the Golden Garland, a painter could not change the main image or the surrounding figures: they must have the same mudras, hand emblems, ceremonial hats, and so forth, and usually the same placement around the central figure. Also constant in the Golden Garland depictions was the positioning of a yidam deity above and a protector below the central figure. What could be changed are the details of the landscape—how the clouds, mountains, rivers, and trees are painted—which animals are depicted, and importantly, the range of color and its tones. Therefore, even though the main elements are the same, it's possible to differentiate schools of painting and sometimes to identify the individual styles of well-known painters. Compare, for example, Lama Rigzin's image of Marpa

Lotsāwa on page 39 with the one painted by his teacher Lhadri Sönam Nyima on page 242.

In the case of Lama Rigzin, one can see Menri elements in the way he paints the blue-green crags, some of the curling cloud formations, the high horizons, the (often symbolic) rippling patterns on bodies of water, and the subtle exuberance of richer colors and the contrast they provide. The Gardri elements are reflected in the delicate, transparent nimbus of the main and some of the secondary figures. These translucent colors are also found in the two spiraling rainbows that rise from the landscape, intertwine, and open out to frame the images of the yidam deities that again radiate rainbow lights, reminding practitioners that these objects of meditation are not solid but made of intangible light. The Gardri style is also found in the indigo outlining of clouds and in the sense of spaciousness, created by the white blushes at the edges of the meadowed areas where they meet other elements (the central throne, the lamas, rocks, and clouds) and by the generous use of white in the painting of the mountains. In this way the empty white space, whence the whole image arises, is present in even what we experience as the most solid—earth and mountains. In sum, one could say that Lama Rigzin's style is a fusion of Gardri and Menri, which was found often enough in Eastern Tibet that it could be known as Khamri, the painting style of Eastern Tibet.

Through interviews and questions, Lama Rigzin has provided a brief history of his lineage, which intertwines with the lives of the Karmapa and the Kagyü masters. Lama Rigzin's teacher was the famous master Lhadri Sönam Nyima (*Lha bris bsod nams nyi ma*, 1921–2000), who at the age of nine entered the Dzapagön (*Dza pa dgon*) monastery of Drupwang Sangyé Tenzin. Here the fledgling artist studied under the tutelage of the renowned Margo Thupten (*Dmar mgo thub bstan*), a monk and hidden yogi who painted in both the Gardri and Menri styles. Sönam

Nyima studied with him for many years and became a consummate artist in both these traditions. (Sönam Nyima's lineage is explained in a book of paintings by his two sons, Tsewang Nyima and Orgyen Lama, with an introduction by Khenpo Chime Rigzin.)

After Sönam Nyima mastered this style with Margo Thupten, he studied how to create and work with paints made of precious stones, which requires special training and experience. Sönam Nyima then traveled to Surmang Monastery in Eastern Tibet where he stayed for many years, painting for the Drukpa Tulku Chökyi Nyima. During this time, the Second Jamgön Kongtrul, Palden Khyentsé Öser (1904–53), was invited to Surmang to bestow the series of empowerments and reading transmissions known as the *Rinchen Terzö* (*Treasury of Precious Termas*). For these, Sönam Nyima painted the small images of the deities known as *wangtsak* (*dbang tsag*), which are used during the empowerments. They so pleased Khyentsé Öser that he invited Sönam Nyima to his residence, Tsadra Rinchen Drak near Palpung Monastery, to paint a copy of the famous Kagyü Sungenma, which was now kept there. Khyentsé Öser said that Sönam Nyima was not an ordinary painter, but one born to paint through his previous karma.

For more than three years, Sönam Nyima stayed with Khyentsé Öser painting copies of the Sungenma while the originals were displayed next to him. Following the custom of painting as a combined effort of artists with different capabilities, Sönam Nyima worked together with Tanglha Tsewang (*Thang lha tshe dbang*, 1902–89), a renowned painter from Dergé, who helped in laying out the proportional lines for the images and in painting the first layers of color along with their shading. As the senior artist, Sönam Nyima took care of the more difficult parts. He made the line drawings to delineate all the elements in the picture. On top of the initial areas of color, he drew the colored and flowing lines that bring the images to life, making them clear and detailed—the most challenging part of the painting, requiring a steady and fluid hand. Finally, he painted the eyes, the door to the inner world of the figure.

While Sönam Nyima was painting these thangkas, the young Sixteenth Karmapa Rangjung Rigpe Dorje visited Tsadra and said about Sönam Nyima's paintings that if they were consecrated it would be good, but if they were not, there would be no difference in the blessing they bestowed; they would be naturally consecrated. This high praise greatly pleased Khyentsé Öser, who was a son of the previous Karmapa.

When Lama Rigzin was still in Tibet, he heard about thangkas of the Golden Garland of the Kagyü Masters, which were kept at Dilyak Monastery in Nangchen, Eastern Tibet. He traveled there and traced a pencil copy of the images' outlines, which he showed to Sönam Nyima who then made corrections in black ink. This is the set that became the basis for the outlines of the paintings in the main shrine hall at Thrangu Tashi Yangtse. Using a special method for transferring these images to the wall, Lama Rigzin placed a large piece of glass on top of each copy of the black ink drawings and traced the outline in black on the glass. A light was shown through the glass to project the image onto the wall, thus assuring that the proportions would be exact. Assistant painters drew the image in pencil and then Lama Rigzin spent some days refining it.

Another shift in tradition occurred to accommodate the space of the shrine hall, which created the three main differences from the usual presentations of these figures in thangkas. In the front of the shrine hall, the space flanking the altar is larger than all the other areas for the murals. On the wall to the altar's right side is Telopa and immediately next to him is Marpa. Usually Hevajra and his consort are depicted above Marpa, but in this case they have been shifted to a space above the neighboring Telopa. Similarly, Naropa occupies the space on the altar's left side and next to him is Milarepa. Mahāmāyā with consort is usually depicted above Milarepa, but this image has been shifted over from Milarepa to the neighboring Naropa. Finally instead of his usual position as Lord of the Family above Mahākāla's head, the Second Karmapa Karma Pakṣi is placed above the doorway of the shrine hall to the right of Mahākāla.

Photographs of the originals were not available as a reference for the color since they had been destroyed during the Cultural Revolution. However, at Tsadra Rinchen Drak, a very clever lay woman hid Sönam Nyima's copies in the hollow of a tree to preserve them. Now kept at Palpung Monastery, these were photographed and reproduced in Taiwan. Another set of paintings, also based on the Sungenma, was given by the 9th Sangyé Nyenpa Rinpoché (1897–1961) to the Sixteenth Karmapa and kept at his monastery in Rumtek, Sikkim. Also photographed and reproduced in Taiwan, they, too, served as the basis for the murals at Thrangu Tashi Yangtse. One of these paintings could often been seen suspended on the scaffolding next to an assistant painter as the line drawings were filled with radiant color.

In March of 2009, the actual painting of the murals at Thrangu Tashi Yangtse began, and they were finished in April of 2012. Over these years, thirty to forty painters sat on a two-story scaffolding set up next to the walls and worked under the tall lights that illuminated the emerging images. Lama Rigzin supervised and taught the artists, many of whom had worked with him in Sarnath, India, to paint murals of the sixteen arhats in the shrine hall of Thrangu Rinpoche's Vajra Vidya Institute. Lama Rigzin was responsible in both places for the refinement of the initial line drawings, the flowing lines that brought definition to the areas of color, and for the final touch, the eyes.

During the painting, at the front of the shrine hall sat a long table full of vibrant hues, set off by the glistening white circles of the mortars and pestles, where the paints were ground from precious stones. Thrangu Rinpoche had especially requested these paints as they give subtler hues, last for hundreds of years, and work well (literally, "become friends") with the brilliance of the gold overlay. These special stones were not available in Nepal and had to be brought from Tibet. Every day the paints were ground and some, such as gold and silver, took many hours to make. Each color required a separate brush, and since the stone paints are hard on brushes, they had to be remade every week in all sizes down to very fine brushes of a few hairs.

This meticulous level of detail can also be found throughout the paintings, from the subtle design on a diaphanous scarf floating in space to a bird flying through the double aura around the Karmapa's head, one part of the bird shadowed by the aura's color and the other not. There is playfulness, too, as the branches of a tree in the painting of Karma Pakṣi curve around to spell out *Karmapa Khyenno* ("Karmapa, know me"). The more one looks at the paintings, the more special they become. In addition to their beauty, they are a reference for practitioners, who can see depictions of the Karmapa and the main Kagyü yidam deities, and also for students of the Karma Kamtsang's history. These special murals of the five forefathers and the sixteen Karmapas will remain a treasure of Thrangu Tashi Yangtse for centuries to come.

Michele Martin
Namo Buddha, Nepal

Part One

The Illustrated Lives of the Five Kagyü Forefathers

Introduction

Vajradhara, Telopa, Naropa,
Marpa, Milarepa, Gampopa,
and the Buddha, Gyalwang Karmapa,
to the lamas of this Golden Garland,
one after the other, I bow.
The pervasive expanse of phenomena, radiant clarity,
this essential mind is the buddha nature.
The lama's inexpressible experience is revealed.
Directly signaling, displaying it clearly
in ways that attune with the times,
the glorious lama plays
in the lotus garden of my heart.

To the five Kagyü forefathers and to the Golden Garland of the successive incarnations of the Buddha Gyalwang Karmapa I offer brilliant white flowers whose abundant petals are these words of offering. Practicing the six yogas of Naropa (the path of method) and mahāmudrā (the path of liberation), you have come to the royal seat of nonmeditation, the dharmakāya. With deep faith I make this offering through the three gates of my body, speech, and mind. I bow at the dust from the stainless feet of these genuine lamas of the flawless practice lineage, who embody an unending flow of blessings.

So that the seed of a perfectly pure faith in this lineage may flourish in our mind streams, I offer these brief spiritual biographies of the five Kagyü forefathers and the Gyalwang Karmapas. In actuality, the life stories of their body, speech, mind, qualities, and activities are inconceivable and beyond the scope of our ordinary minds. As Candrakīrti states in *Entering the Middle Way*:

> It's not for the lack of spacious sky that birds turn back;
> it's because their strength has come to an end.
> Likewise, the bodhisattvas, hearers, and solitary realizers turn back
> from telling of the Buddha's qualities, infinite like space. (10.41)

If a bird flies into the sky's expanse and then returns to the earth, it is not because space was used up and the bird could not find a place to go; it has to return because it came to the limit of the strength in its own wings. Likewise, even if the Buddha were to bless this world with his presence for uncountable kalpas, the Buddha himself could not recount all of his qualities. Further, if the bodhisattvas abiding on their various levels cannot express the Buddha's qualities just as they are, how could we ordinary beings do so? So here, we will take up a mere drop from the ocean of life stories that these protectors of living beings displayed for the sake of ordinary individuals. The purpose of these accounts is to develop devotion and faith within our minds.

Why is faith important? Generally, faith precedes any positive action that we might perform. In particular, when we are relying on a lama as our spiritual friend, or when we are engaged in listening, reflecting, and meditating on the genuine Dharma, faith is extremely important. The *Sutra of the Ten Dharmas* states:

For those who lack faith,
virtuous qualities will not arise,
just as a green sprout will not grow
from a seed burned by fire.

And from the *Noble Sutra of the Vast Play*:

> The Buddha said, "Ānanda, you should engender faith. This is what the tathāgatas request us to do."

Especially when we are practicing in the Secret Mantrayāna, faith and devotion are crucial. Whether or not our Dharma practice goes well depends on whether or not blessings have entered our mind stream. The lama is the root of blessings, so whether we receive these blessings or not depends on our lama. It is not certain, however, that blessings will come to us through the lama's mere presence. Receiving them depends on two things: an authentic lama with the ability to transfer blessings to a specific disciple, and a disciple with faith and devotion. If we have great faith and devotion, we will receive great blessings; if our faith and devotion are middling, the blessings will be middling; and if we have only slight faith and devotion, the blessings of the genuine Dharma will be slight as well. As the Drikung Kyopa Jikten Sumgön explains:

If the sun of devotion does not shine
on the snow mountain of the lama's four kāyas,
the river of blessings will not flow,
so engender true devotion in your mind.

Furthermore, when we are engaged in the uncommon preliminary practices, there is a reason for the need to practice guru yoga with great diligence. Why? Because this brings faith and devotion that allow us to see our present and lineage lamas as actual buddhas. Bengar Jampal Sangpo writes in his Vajradhara Lineage Prayer:

> Devotion is the head of meditation as is taught.
> The lamas open the gate to the treasury of oral instruction.
> To this meditator who is continually supplicating,
> grant your blessings that uncontrived devotion may arise within.

Faith and devotion resemble the head of meditation. Among the many parts of our body, we value our head the most. Likewise, when we are practicing any kind of genuine Dharma, faith is critical, and in practicing in the Secret Mantrayāna, it is especially important that we see our lama as a buddha in person. Traditionally, it is said that the root of blessing is the lama; the root of accomplishment (or siddhi) is the yidam deity; and the root of activity is the Dharma protectors. We can also meditate on the lama as embodying all Three Roots, as is explained in the *Cakrasaṃvara Tantra*:

> The lama is the Buddha, the lama is the Dharma,
> and the lama is the Sangha as well:
> the lama is the creator of everything.

The lama's heart-mind is the Buddha; the lama's speech is the genuine Dharma; and the lama's body is the Sangha. With fully focused faith and devotion, we should recognize that the lama embodies the very nature of the Three Jewels.

The best method for generating faith and devotion in our present lama and lineage lamas is to know about them through their spiritual biographies. So we should read and listen to them, explain them to others, and bring them to mind again and again. In making a real connection, we can develop devotion from the depths of our hearts. By recalling the hardships that previous lamas underwent for the sake of the Dharma, we will not let ourselves remain in an ordinary, uninspired state. But, thinking, "I will train in the genuine Dharma come what may," we will be delighted to practice and be able to bring forth real devotion. This is truly important.

1. Lord Telopa
2. Gyepa Dorjé and Dakmema
3. Khorlo Demchok and Dorjé Phakmo
4. Rikden Khandro
5. Jetsün Khölpoga

Lord Telopa Sherap Sangpo

10th–11th c.

Serving Dharima and pounding sesame seeds,
you found supreme siddhi and emptied
the country of Sahor completely.
I bow at the feet of the powerful yogi Telo.

The *Ocean of Dākiṇīs Tantra* has this to say about Lord Telopa:

Long after the Buddha taught,
you were a yogi of the Vajrayāna,
grinding sesame and famous as Sherap Sangpo.
Protector of beings, the Buddha himself has come.

The *Cakrasaṃvara Tantra* states:

Telo is the Buddha, the protector of beings.
In particular he's the true wheel of supreme bliss—
Cakrasaṃvara, utmost bliss.

Further, when Telopa went to Ogyen in the west, the wisdom ḍākiṇīs said:

> He is Cakrasaṃvara, father of
> all the buddhas of the three times.
> Even if the sky poured down a hail
> of vajras, he could not be conquered.

In line with these quotes, it was revealed in many tantras that Telopa is actually Cakrasaṃvara.

In the land of Jagora, a part of the country of Sahor in the southeastern part of India, Telopa was born to his father, the great Brahmin Rabsal (Completely Clear), and his mother, a Brahmin named Salwa (Clarity). During his birth, many wondrous signs occurred, and brilliant light radiated from all directions. For this reason, they named their son Salwai Ö (Clear Light). His sister was called Saldrön (Clear Lamp). His parents summoned a person skilled in augury, who examined the small boy intently for a long time. Since a variety of signs occurred that pointed to a human, a deity, a naga, or a buddha, the seer could not determine outright what the signs of this emanation indicated and did not have the courage to make a correct prophecy. Filled with wonder, he gave the infant the same name as his parents did, Salwai Ö.

After this, the child was prevented from traveling near or far, and aside from his parents, no one else was allowed to see him. They nurtured his development, and the amount another child would grow in one year, he exceeded in one month; the amount another child would grow in one month, he exceeded in one day.

Once, in an isolated place, his mother was sitting with her back to the sun while she affectionately played with him, murmuring sweet words and giving him nourishing food. Suddenly a fearsome shadow appeared and covered the upper part of the child. When his mother looked back, she saw an old woman with thirty-six ugly signs. Terrified, his mother said, "Don't stay here. Go away!"

The old woman replied in verse:

> Though you hold him with affection,
> not one place on earth is free of death.

"Then what should he do?" his mother asked.

> "Tend buffalo and learn his letters.
> The ḍākiṇīs will give a prophecy."

With these words, the woman disappeared. The parents understood this to be a ḍākiṇī's prediction. When the boy had reached the age of one, he was the size of a thirteen-year-old. The father took him together with their buffalo into the middle of the woods. There when the child was leaning against the trunk of an aloe wood tree, looking after the buffalo and studying his letters, the ugly woman reappeared: "Child, what are the names of your parents, your sister, yourself, and this tree? Why are you watching buffalo? What's the use of studying those letters?"

The boy answered: "This country is eastern Jagora. My father is the Brahmin Rabsal, and my mother, the Brahmin Salwa. My sister is named Rabsé Saldrön. I am called Salwai Ö. The tree is aloe wood. The buffalo are our family's primary wealth. Through letters, I search for the conventional meaning."

The woman got angry: "All those answers are plain wrong!"

"OK, what do you say?" the boy asked.

She replied in verse:

> This country is not eastern Jagora, but western Ogyen,
> the central place.
> Your father is not the Brahmin Rabsal, but Cakrasaṃvara, great bliss.
> Your mother is not the Brahmin Salwa, but Vajrayoginī, mother
> of the sugatas.
> Your sister is not Rabsé Saldrön, but me who gives you bliss.
> You are not the boy Salwai Ö, but Vajradhara, the sovereign
> of all families.
> This tree trunk is not aloe wood, but the supreme wish-fulfilling tree that
> grants all wishes.
> These buffalo are not your family's primary wealth, but as you tend them,
> meditative experience will fulfill your hopes and wishes.
> Don't seek the ultimate in conventional letters; they point to the
> whispered lineage beyond words.

The boy asked, "How do you search for the whispered lineage?" She replied again in verse:

> It is found in the place of the dākiṇīs from Ogyen.
> You're a master holding samaya and a prophecy;
> if you want to receive this lineage, you can.

When she finished speaking, her ugly aspect vanished, and she appeared as a ravishing young woman. At just this, the young boy realized the reality of his mind and rose up into the sky, where he gave a discourse filled with deep meaning.

Right afterward, he displayed numerous emanations all at once. From among these, one became like a son to Gelongma Til Tsongma. This one emanation took monk's vows and received the name Sherap Sangpo (Excellent Wisdom). The brother of Til Tsongma was a monk and an elder in the Sangha, so he looked after the young monk. Sherap Sangpo naturally grew into adulthood and was very skilled in reading texts.

One day, it happened that a very beautiful, attractive young woman said to him, "Young boy, you should act like a madman," and then she vanished. So Sherap Sangpo threw all the texts from the roof of the main shrine hall. The monks said, "He's gone crazy," and put him in iron chains, which he wore while practicing for six years. Then the elder monk set him free and let him do as he wished. With this monk acting as the abbot, the young man took full ordination and received the name Gelong Kalapa.

Then he killed many locusts by severing their heads from their bodies and heaping them up into two different piles. When he was going to eat, people severely criticized him. One time, when the king was traveling to a great ceremony, he saw all of this and asked, "Why do you, who have the appearance of a venerable monk, kill so many creatures?" Gelong Kalapa snapped his fingers—the insects' bodies and heads reconnected, and they flew off into the sky. This inspired great faith in the king and his retinue.

Another of the emanations went to Ogyen and requested the Three Cycles of the Jewel, belonging to the whispered lineage, and also the Nine Cycles of the Formless

Dākiṇīs. When he was leaving Ogyen, soaring in the sky like a king of birds, the dākiṇīs supplicated Telopa to stay in Ogyen. He responded:

> For the benefit of three sons—Naro, Riri, and Kasori—
> to the monastery of Tsugi Norbu,
> Sherap Sangpo goes free of hindrance
> like a bird flying through space.

With these words he departed. At that time a disembodied voice said, "I taught the Nine Cycles of the Formless Dākiṇīs. Understand the three sons to be Naropa, Riripa, and Kasoripa." Another emanation heard the Dharma from Vajradhara in person.

Of the two transmissions of Telopa—the shorter and the longer lineages— the first is the transmission of the shorter lineage. When the lord Telopa was residing in the cemetery called the Kiri Mass of Blazing Fire and nurturing his experience and realization, Vajradhara, the enjoyment body of the Buddha, revealed himself directly to Telopa and gave him empowerments, blessings, and the teachings of the entire Dharma of the Secret Mantra. Telopa attained mastery over the complete instructions of the four classes of tantra.

The way Telopa served the lamas of the four transmissions shows how he received the longer transmissions. When people asked Telopa, "Which lamas did you serve to attain accomplishment?" Telopa replied, "Telopa has no human teacher. My lama is the Omniscient One." But people did not believe or have faith in him, so in order to change this, he demonstrated the manner of relying on lamas who held the four transmissions.

Telopa himself affirmed:

> Nāgārjuna, Cārya, Lawapa,
> and the Fortunate Lady are my lamas
> for the four transmissions.

As explained in Jamgön Kongtrül's *Treasury of Knowledge*, Telopa received from Cāryapa (also called Kṛṣṇācārya or Ngakpo Chöpa) the transmission of caṇḍālī (inner heat); from Nāgārjuna, the transmissions of the illusory body and luminosity; from Lawapa, the transmission of dream yoga; and from the Fortunate Lady (Sukhasiddhi) the transmissions of bardo practice and transference.

Subsequently, he became the servant of Dharima and emptied the country of Sahor in the following way. The powerful yogi Mataṅgi made a prophecy:

> In the center of a city in the country of Sahor to the east, Vajrayoginī will reveal herself as a prostitute called Dharima with a retinue of five hundred. Be her attendant and maintain your realization of the path. It will not be long before you attain the supreme siddhi of mahāmudrā, through which many living beings will be liberated.

So Telopa followed his advice and went to her. By day he worked pounding sesame seeds and by night, he worked escorting the customers of Dharima and doing other tasks. By sustaining his realization for twelve years, he attained the supreme siddhi of mahāmudrā and united with a wisdom ḍākiṇī. He sang a song of realization to Dharima, and she became inseparable from the main wisdom ḍākiṇī. They remained in the sky at the height of seven plantain trees, while Telopa sang this song, a vajra doha, illuminating his work of pounding sesame seeds.

Emaho! Sesame oil is the essence of the seed.
Though you know this, your minds are clouded.
Not seeing the twelve interdependent links,
you cannot extract the essence—the sesame's oil.
The wisdom of the coemergent natural state
abides forever in the heart of every living being,
but stays unrealized until the lama points it out.
When sesame is pounded, the husks come free
and the essence, sesame oil, appears.
Like this, the lama reveals what suchness is,
clarifies that it's like the oil in sesame seeds.
Since they have the same essential nature, objects are inseparable.
Kyeho! What was long in coming and difficult to plumb
is realized right now. How wondrous!

As he sang this doha in a very pleasant melody, all the inhabitants of Sahor—from the king, ministers, queens, and important people to the birds in the sky, wild animals on the earth, and mice underground—were liberated in an instant. They all rose into the sky and the great city was emptied out. Afterward, Sherap Sangpo became famous as Telopa.

Some of Telopa's emanations cared for eight heart sons, all of whom had the name Yogi.

(1) In one region, there lived King Dawa Sengé. In order not to transgress his mother's word, he arranged an extensive feast offering (*gaṇacakra*). While the yogi Nuden Dorjé was presiding over the feast, Lord Telopa arrived riding the sun and

moon. He took the yogi under his care and revealed many miraculous things, such as infinite deities and their mandalas appearing in each pore of his body.

(2) At the glorious monastery of Nālandā, the pandita Nakpo, who was not a Buddhist, was trying to destroy the Buddhist teachings. Telopa competed with him for prowess in debate and magic. Victorious, Telopa matured him through the Dharma, and the pandita became known as Yogi Nakpo Gewa.

(3) A great king was living in Bengal in eastern India. A magician, who was well versed in creating illusions, had launched an imaginary army and was stealing the kingdom away. At this time, Telopa turned back the magician's army and then gave him instructions, whereby the magician became Yogi Denpar Mawa.

(4) In Langkapa in eastern India, there lived a haughty barmaid. She received key instructions from Telopa and attained siddhi, becoming known as Yoginī Nyima Dzin.

(5) Every day, a man called Jina the King of Butchers killed a huge number of living beings. One day Telopa transformed the meat Jina was cooking into the flesh of his very own son, and this made him stop killing. Telopa then gave Jina instructions that mature and liberate, and he became known as Yogi Dejé, the butcher who attained siddhi.

(6) Telopa debated with a scholar of the non-Buddhist Lokāyata (materialist or nihilist) school and defeated him. Moreover, Telopa made him see directly the karmic results of doing good and evil so the nihilist came to believe in karma and entered the gate of Dharma. He became liberated through receiving instructions from Telopa and was known as Yogi Gawa Dangdenpa.

(7) In another country, Telopa went to see an arrogant singer. Telopa sang a wide repertoire of marvelous songs, some set in this world and others never heard

before—sublime songs, songs of gandharvas (celestial musicians), and songs from the human realm. These he followed with vajra songs that transcended the mind and this world. The proud singer developed faith, and through receiving instruction, he became liberated and was known as Yogi Yangden Kukpa.

(8) A powerful non-Buddhist lived in the region of Pāṭaliputra. If he was the least bit displeased with someone, he would kill that person with sorcery. Hundreds of thousands of people paid him respect. Through the instructions of Telopa, he was liberated and known as Yogi Dawa.

Assuming the form of a fully ordained monk who was peaceful and gentle, Telopa went to the front of the palace belonging to King Sengé Dawa. At one point the king noticed him and, after examining him extensively, the king felt faith in the monk and invited him to the palace. The monk offered the king the sublime Dharma and created many volumes of teachings that were in harmony with Buddhism. The king was completely convinced that this monk was in truth Cakrasaṃvara and told this to others, so that the monk's fame spread.

King Sengé Dawa called together a great number of siddhas, dākas, and dākiṇīs for a Dharma feast and invited Telopa to be the head of the ceremonies (*vajrācārya*). As the great feast was being celebrated, Telopa entered into the samādhis of numerous mandalas, so that some people saw him as Hevajra, others as Cakrasaṃvara or Mahāmāyā, and yet others as Guhyasamāja or Kālacakra—there were so many different ways of seeing him. When the king asked Telopa about this, he replied:

> My body is Hevajra.
> My speech is Mahāmāyā.
> My mind is Cakrasaṃvara.
> My sense faculties are Guhyasamāja.

My main limbs are Red and Black Yamāntaka
and extremities, Vajrabhairava.
The place of my nadis is the Four Vajra Seats;
the place of my prāṇa is the Garland of Vajras,
and my bindus are the Treasury of Secrets.
My ushnisha is the Skull of Śākyamuni;
bliss is the Unity of All the Buddhas.
The very nature of the whole is Kālacakra.
My pores are inseparable from the body, speech, and mind
of the buddhas of all three times.

With these words, Telopa became universally known as the actual buddha, Vajradhara.

In this way, the great siddha led to the place known as the Realm of Enjoying Space a great number of individuals from a vast region. Finally, numerous assemblies of dākas and dākiṇīs welcomed Telopa with immense offerings, and he demonstrated the way of traveling to the Realm of Enjoying Space.

1. Lord Naropa
2. Khachöma
3. Bramsé Kunrik
4. Ḍombhi Heruka
5. Mahāmāyā

The Powerful Naropa

SCHOLAR AND SIDDHA

10th–11th c.

Just as prophesied by the yidams and ḍākiṇīs,
you endured hardship with complete faith in your lama.
Through courageous effort you attained supreme siddhi.
I bow respectfully at the feet of the great scholar Naropa.

In speaking of Naropa, Telopa said:

I am actually Cakrasaṃvara.
My disciple is truly the Buddha—
this noble being, the great scholar Naropa.

And he continued:

Naropa accomplished the dhāraṇī of a perfect memory;
he followed me through twelve arduous trials.
His realization is just the same as mine
so generations to come can rely on him.
If you want realization, follow Naropa.

In a Muslim country to the west, this noble one was born to his father, the king Gewai Gocha, and his mother, Palgyi Lodrö. This was at dawn in the fourth (merit-increasing) month in the year of the Male Fire Dragon. His birth was the occasion of many wondrous signs as thunder roared and the earth trembled. As soon as he was born, the infant nodded his head three times toward the north, signaling that those living in the northern Land of Snow would be his disciples.

When they examined his signs, they found the newborn to be an amazing being. It was prophesied that if he stayed at home, he would become a sovereign with power over a vast territory; if he became ordained, like the king Śuddhodana's son Siddhārtha, he would resemble the Buddha. The infant was given the name Kuntu Sangpo (Excellent in Every Way).

From his young years, the child had great faith, a sharp mind, and perfect knowing, able to comprehend naturally all the traditional areas of study. Although his parents did have respect for and faith in the Dharma, since they had but one son, they feared their family lineage would be broken, so they nurtured in their child the talents that were useful in worldly affairs. Nevertheless, through his inner power the young boy came to know all the qualities of the Dharma. At long last he received his parents' permission and took lay precepts from the Kashmiri abbot Namkha Drakpa, who gave him the name Namkha Nyingpo (Heart of Space). For three years he studied all the fields of knowledge in the traditional great treatises and became a very adept scholar.

The young man was then motivated to take full ordination, and he fervently requested permission from his parents, but they withheld it, so he could not take the vows. His parents urged him to get married, but he refused, so they took an oath to kill themselves. Their son responded, "If there's no other way but to take on a household, then I will need a woman who's like this: not caught up in a lot of concepts, strictly pure, and named Drimema (Stainless Lady). She must be sixteen years old, belong to the Mahāyāna family, and be endowed with compassion, but not be a Buddhist." At this the king became uneasy, thinking that it would be impossible to find such a woman, but one of his ministers said that a woman like this could be found, so the king began a search. Finally, in a city of non-Buddhists they found a young woman with all the requisite qualities, and she became the young man's queen.

Kuntu Sangpo taught the Dharma extensively to his queen, and she developed great faith in him and served him well. One time he told her about his personal history and his desire to take ordination. She supported her master's Dharma practice and said, "Do whatever is best," so the prince received the chance to become a monk.

Without any difficulty he went to the monastery and was given a renunciate's vows by the master Sangyé Kyang, who served as the abbot, while Yeshé Ö was the ritual master. The prince received the new name Sangyé Yeshé (Wisdom of the Buddha). Afterward he traveled again to Kashmir to the monastery of his pandita where, in the midst of the requisite number of monks, he took full ordination with Chökyi Lama as abbot and Chökyi Yeshé as the ritual master. Through studying the three baskets of the Vinaya, Sutra, and Abhidharma along with all the sections of tantra, the young monk developed the power of his mind to the point that he was beyond compare. Chosen as the elder of the monastery Nyangen Mepai Tsal (The Grove Beyond Suffering), he became famous far and wide as the Elder Tenpa Dzinpa (Holder of the Teachings).

At this time the great monastic university of Nālandā was flourishing as the residence of many famous scholars. Pawo Tsuklak Trengwa's *Origins of Dharma: A Feast for the Learned* recounts that the scholar protecting the eastern gate was the master Mithup Dawa; the southern gate was protected by Jetari Draklé Namgyal; and the western gate by the master Nakpo Shapché. Since there was no protector for the northern gate, five hundred scholars met to discuss the situation and decided to install glorious Naropa. No one, Buddhist or non-Buddhist, could defeat him in debate, and he turned many non-Buddhist teachers into Buddhists. Finally Naropa was made the abbot of Nālandā and was given the name Palden Jikmé Drakpa (Glorious One, Fearless and Famous).

Once, when he was reading a text, a terrifying shadow darkened the page. When Naropa looked up, he saw an ugly old woman with just seven teeth.

"What are you looking at?" she queried.

"It's a text from the corpus of the three pitakas and the sections of tantra," he replied.

"Do you understand it?"

"Yes, I do."

"Do you know the words or the meaning?"

"I know the words," he answered.

The old woman laughed with delight, and raising her walking stick up to the sky, she danced.

"And I also know the meaning," Naropa added.

Suddenly sad, the old woman sobbed and struck the ground with her stick.

"Why are you so upset?"

"It's true that you know the words. But to say that you know the meaning is a lie. That makes me miserable."

"Well, then, who knows the meaning?"

"My brother is the only one."

"How can I meet him?"

"Pray to him and you'll meet." With these words she vanished.

Wishing to search for a lama who could teach the inner meaning, the great scholar thought, "No matter what happens, I must leave." So giving up all his belongings—his statues and all his objects for veneration plus his many texts—he departed. The great scholars of Nālandā who defended the gates and all the monks earnestly requested him to stay, but Naropa would not listen and he left, traveling to the east.

Thinking that he would seek his lama through Hevajra, Naropa engaged in the practice of this deity. One day he heard from the sky:

> On a relative level,
> auspicious connections are not all the same.
> Rely on Cakrasaṃvara as you seek
> your lama, the Buddha, and you'll find him.

So Naropa performed the practice of Cakrasaṃvara in a cemetery. At that time, two young women appeared and told him, "You should practice Cakrasaṃvara like this. We directly asked the king Vajradhara about it," and they explained this practice to Naropa. He closed his eyes, and reflecting on the meaning of what they had said, he intuitively understood it and trusted that their words were true. When he opened his eyes, the two young women were nowhere to be seen.

Afterward, in an early morning dream, both of them appeared, saying, "We are ḍākiṇīs who protect this region. Meditate as we have taught you." So Naropa practiced accordingly, and when he had finished one hundred thousand recitations of Cakrasaṃvara's seven-syllable mantra, the earth shook, lights radiated in the sky, and a lovely fragrance appeared. These and other unusual signs actually happened.

Then Naropa heard a voice say, "You have a close relationship with Telopa from the east." So with his mind completely focused on Telopa, Naropa traveled to the east for a number of days, undergoing numerous hardships that brought him to the brink of despair. Again from the sky, he heard a voice that spurred him on: "Do not heed the demon, this villain of laziness. Seek the Buddha Telopa in the east." This roused Naropa's courage and he made a solemn oath: "From this day onward, without regard for life or limb, I will face any difficulty in order to find my lama Telopa." And so he continued his journey eastward.

Supplicating intensely as he traveled, Naropa arrived at a footpath so narrow only one person could pass through. Here he came upon a destitute female leper who had no legs and stumps for arms.

"Let me by," he said.

"If you're in a hurry, step over me," she replied. "If not, take another route." So Naropa covered his nose with his hand and stepped over her. She remarked:

> Bound in concepts, you're wrapped up tight.
> How could you find your lama this way?
> Only the immature are stuck
> in positing "pure" and "impure."

Then everything—the female leper, the narrow path, and all the rest—disappeared, and he found himself in an empty desert.

This was the first of Naropa's twelve minor trials. In all, he went through twelve major and twelve minor trials, which are explained at length in other accounts of his life. These stories relate events that run counter to the usual ways of the world. In general, when people read these remarkable narratives (which can be rather frightening), there is a danger that they might take them in the wrong way and doubt that the accounts are true. To avoid this, a reader should be certain that the lama depicted is truly the Buddha and that it is due to their own obscurations and negative actions that they cannot see the lama as they actually are.

Further, a variety of unpleasant figures can appear in the spiritual biographies, such as a poverty-stricken woman with leprosy or a maggot-infested dog, and also shocking actions, such as killing one's parents or washing the insides of a living person. For example, the noble Asaṅga devoted himself to the practice of Maitreya for twelve long years without meeting him. Then he encountered a miserably infected dog that was actually a manifestation of Maitreya. Intense compassion for her arose within Asaṅga, and through its power his obscurations were eliminated; only then could he see Maitreya directly. Thus, it is commonly taught that what we are able to perceive depends on how obscured we are.

During Naropa's twelve minor trials as well, a variety of sights appeared to him. They were not just random incidents but profound instructions revealed through symbols, all of which should be understood as sublime key instructions. For example, washing the insides of a person is an analogy for washing away the stains of the afflictions in our mindstream. Killing parents signifies that we should eliminate attachment and hatred, which, like our mother and father, cause birth in samsara. In this way, once we know how to combine the symbol with the meaning it reveals, it is essential that we open our hearts to genuine faith in these accounts of the masters.

After Naropa's eleventh minor trial, he became completely discouraged, for he had met emanations of his lama but was not fortunate enough to be accepted as a disciple. So thinking that his body, the result of maturing karma, had become an obstacle, he made this aspiration: "Tossing off this body, may I meet my lama in the bardo." As he began to slit his throat with a razor, he saw Telopa before him, brilliant in a sphere of rainbow light and displaying the mudra of giving protection. Prostrating with faith so powerful he could hardly bear it, Naropa supplicated Telopa, reciting his litany of woes.

Telopa replied, "Not separate for one moment, I have been with you from the very first, from the time you saw the female leper up until now. Due to your own obscurations you saw me in different forms: sometimes as a female dog, sometimes as a fisherman, a hunter, someone killing his parents, and others—a whole assortment of impure beings. Now, through your devotion that's ready to give up even this life, you have purified the obscurations of your negative karma and can see me as I am." With these words, Telopa descended to the ground and revealed in succession the twelve symbolic empowerments that matured the mind of Naropa.

After this Naropa underwent the twelve major trials:

1. When Telopa was residing in a certain region, Naropa prostrated, circumambulated, and made a mandala offering. He then asked Telopa to give him instruction. Telopa abruptly got up and went to the very top of a temple that had thirteen stories. He said, "If I had a disciple, he would leap from here." Naropa jumped without hesitation and landed hard on the ground, breaking his arms, legs, and skull, leaving him with just a trace of his life force. Though about to expire, Naropa was happy, thinking that his death was meaningful since it happened while carrying out his lama's command. Telopa then came to him and rubbed an ointment on Naropa, saying, "There's nothing wrong with you." At that moment, Naropa became more handsome than ever and discovered new meditative experience and realization.

2. Telopa took a rigid bamboo scalpel with the sharpest point and pierced Naropa's body front to back many times. But the moment Telopa touched him, Naropa's body had not so much as a scar, and Naropa then followed his lama everywhere.
3. Telopa made Naropa build a bridge over a deep swamp filled with leeches and forcefully threw him into this pit of ooze. The leeches and other creatures bored holes in Naropa's body and drank all his blood. When he was completely depleted, Telopa soothed Naropa with his hand, and he became better than before.
4. Telopa put Naropa in the middle of fires so that he was completely surrounded by flames. All of his skin and muscles were consumed by the inferno while his brains, spinal cord, blood, and lymph all dried up. He was at his end when Telopa rubbed him with his hand, and Naropa became even more attractive than previously.
5. Naropa scooped up food and drink from a lavish gathering to give Telopa, and a large group of the guests beat him to a pulp. When he was on the verge of dying, Telopa stroked him with his hand, and Naropa was restored to his former body.
6. One queen of a certain king was staying in the forest. Telopa told Naropa, "You must say to her, 'All alone you should come away with me. If you won't, I'll forcibly carry you off.'" Her eunuchs were incensed and beat Naropa mercilessly. Thinking he had died, they threw him away. The moment Telopa rubbed Naropa, his body turned beautiful and blissful.
7. At Telopa's command, Naropa grabbed the hand of a minister's wife and, pulling her down from her seat, started to lead her away. The minister and his attendants were outraged. They broke all his limbs and tossed his body

away. Naropa had but a speck of his life-force left when Telopa touched him and restored Naropa to his former self.

8. At a crossroads, Naropa flung a garland of flowers around the neck of a bejeweled bride-to-be. Those who had come to greet her pummeled Naropa and hurled him a long distance away. By a mere touch, Telopa brought Naropa to supreme bliss.
9. First, Telopa made him take a wife, and then he made Naropa give him the woman. Telopa said, "Your penis finds this young woman attractive," and then he beat Naropa's male member until blood flowed copiously. Again, just by the lama's touch, Naropa was healed.
10. Trying to catch up, Naropa ran after a walker, but the person kept getting farther and farther away. Naropa became utterly exhausted and passed out. When he had but a modicum of consciousness and his breath was on the verge of stopping, Telopa stroked him, and Naropa knew great bliss.
11. Naropa let his own blood and sprinkled it over the earth. Using a sharp weapon to cut off his limbs and toes, he used them to make the heaps of offerings in a mandala. As soon as Telopa placed his hands on the crown of Naropa's head (the central heap of the mandala), Naropa's body became very handsome and radiant.
12. Telopa created the appearance of being slightly angry. He struck Naropa in the face with his shoe, and vigorously booted Naropa in the chest saying, "I've showed you so much, and you don't understand." With this Naropa's mind went elsewhere. When he recovered from fainting, he felt that all the abandonments, realizations, and qualities of Telopa's lineage had been conveyed to him. Telopa sang this verse:

Kyé ho! This is naturally aware, primordial wisdom;
it transcends all speech and all objects of mental experience.
I, Telopa, have nothing whatever to teach;
you must know through revealing yourself to yourself.

In this way, through the twelve major trials Telopa introduced Naropa to mind's abiding nature, just as it is, and also gave him key instructions, too numerous to count, about the essence of the definitive meaning. More detailed explanations of these trials can be found in other texts.

In reading the accounts of Naropa's many trials, we learn of his great persistence and forbearance of hardship, and also of Telopa's immense powers and abilities. Further, these stories show what a real disciple is. Believing fully that the lama is truly the Buddha, a disciple is able to sustain pure vision in relation to whatever the lama might do. The disciple takes whatever the lama might say to be valid, and does not disregard even the smallest part. In order to follow the lama's direction, a true (and very advanced) disciple is able to sacrifice even their own life. While fulfilling the lama's commands, a disciple is able to engage their complete body, speech, and mind without a hair's tip of a thought for themselves.

The purpose of learning about the life stories of past lamas, therefore, is not just to hear some amazing tales. These life stories should be taken as models for our own lives so that we emulate what we find meaningful and essential. It is important to connect with the life stories through our own experience. Developing the ability to generate great faith and pure vision, a disciple should follow the lama's words exactly. Avoiding any distractions of this mundane life related to body, speech, or mind, a disciple engages in genuine Dharma practice. If we can extract what is essential from our life, we will have achieved the purpose of reading these life stories.

Since Naropa attained realization and liberated his own mind stream, Telopa gave him permission to spread the teachings. Led by his compassion, Naropa taught others and matured their mind streams. He went to the country of the king Sengé Dawa and displayed a variety of miracles, which created great faith in the king and many others. Naropa gave them instructions about the abiding nature of mind, and established them on the correct path to awakening. Then he returned to Nālandā and again defended its northern gate against debaters from the outside. Naropa benefited countless living beings throughout his life and spread the precious teachings widely throughout his life. For fortunate disciples, he bestowed the essential truth of the Secret Mantrayāna.

Important for the history of Dharma in Tibet was the connection between Naropa and Marpa Lotsāwa, the Tibetan who spent a total of sixteen years and seven months in India under the tutelage of this great master. Like water flowing into water, Naropa gave to Marpa the six yogas from the path of method and also tantras, such as Hevajra and Cakrasaṃvara, as well as all his experiential and oral instructions. Finally, Naropa traveled to the Realm of Enjoying Space.

At this time, Marpa was in Tibet, and even though he was advanced in years, without regard for the difficulties, he gladly took up the task of returning to India. For three long months Marpa pleaded from his heart, supplicating his lama, and finally Naropa revealed himself. The lama and disciple went together to Bodh Gaya (the Vajra Seat) and to Pullahari. During this time, Naropa gave Marpa the complete oral and experiential instructions related to the whispered lineage of the ḍākiṇīs, as well as the transference of consciousness to another, and other practices. At the end Naropa said, "Son, I empower you as my regent in Tibet, the northern Land of Snow." Placing his hand on Marpa's head, Naropa sang this song:

Marpa, Translator from Tibet,
you carry the past karma of correctly purifying your mind.
You hold the jewel of a universal monarch,
and, turned from samsara, you write your words in stone.

Your family lineage will fade like a flower in the sky;
your Dharma lineage will run longer than a mighty river.
Like the offspring of lions and garuḍas,
disciples will come, each one better than the last.

To condense the essential meaning of the Mahāyāna:
it matures and liberates the karmically connected.
You are the king of fortunate disciples to be trained,
bringing them into the kingdom of Dharma.

Now go to the central part of Tibet
lying to the north in that land of snow,
adorned with varieties of fragrant trees
and tall slopes covered in medicinal forests.

There you'll find fortunate disciples, good vessels.
Son, your goals will be fulfilled.
When you have passed from this life,
in the place of great bliss, the equal nature,
we'll meet once more in radiant clarity.

Then music resonated throughout the sky, and a lovely fragrance drifted through the air. Uncountable light rays, more numerous than the sun's and moon's, filled all space, and assemblies of offering deities gathered in crowds. In their midst, seated on a lion throne and layered lotus flowers, was the great lama Naropa. Inconceivable numbers of dākiṇīs and dākas were prostrating and circumambulating him, making offerings and giving praise. Then Naropa rose to greater and greater heights as he moved into the expanse of the sky and departed for the Realm of Enjoying Space.

1. Marpa Lotsāwa
2. Metön Sönam Gyaltsen
3. Tsurtön Wang Ngé
4. Yum Dakmema
5. Ngok Chöku Dorjé
6. Düsölma

Marpa Lotsāwa Chökyi Lodrö

THE KING OF TRANSLATORS

1000–1085

> You took the scholar Naropa as your spiritual friend,
> and in the Cool Land you lit the lamp
> of the teachings—an ocean of tantras.
> I bow at the feet of Marpa Lotsāwa, the king of translators.

Marpa Lotsāwa Chökyi Lodrö was born as the third of five sons to his father, Marpa Wangchuk Öser, and his mother, Gyalmo Lodrö. While he was still in the womb, his mother had many auspicious dreams: she held up a butter lamp that cleared all the darkness from the world; the sound of a resonant conch shell filled a billion worlds; the sun and moon rose and appeared in front of her breasts. In Tashi Lingpa, situated in upper Könchok (a part of upper Besar within Lhodrak), the child was born amid wondrous signs during the year of the Iron Mouse (1000) into a family lineage named Marpa.

From the age of twelve, he studied with a Nyingma scholar and learned to read and write without difficulty. Then along the way Marpa became wild and unruly. His relatives thought that he would cause legal troubles inside and outside the family, so they agreed that it would be good to send him into the Dharma.

At the age of fifteen, Marpa gave all his belongings to Drokmi Lotsāwa, but the master would not give him Dharma teachings in return. So he learned the colloquial language of India from yogis who were staying nearby, and he studied Sanskrit with Drokmi Lotsāwa for three years, becoming an expert. Since Marpa was not receiving Dharma teachings, he thought of going to India and said to his relatives, "If I die in terrible pain for the sake of the Dharma, it's all right. In India I will meet authentic lamas who are scholars and realized masters. I will seek profound oral instructions from them." So he sold all he had for gold and departed to India.

First, he stopped to stay a few days at Kyirong and supplicate the Noble Wati (a statue of Avalokiteśvara). He gave a few Dharma teachings on abandoning negative actions, performing positive ones, and taking refuge, which gave people faith and interest in the Dharma. Afterward he crossed the mountains into Nepal and stayed for three years to get used to the heat. Marpa studied the practices of The Four Seats and the protectress Düsölma (Dhūmavatī) with the Nepali Chitherpa, and he also received the empowerment of Hevajra. Then Marpa journeyed to Lakshetra in the west and received teachings on the Kriya and Üpa tantras. When a feast offering was performed there, four yogis skilled in miraculous displays participated. One came riding a jackal and another was riding a cat. "Who are they?" Marpa asked. "They're all disciples of Naropa," was the reply. Marpa experienced great joy and felt a blessing just from hearing the name of Naropa. With faith in the four yogis, Marpa offered each one some gold and requested key instructions from each of them.

Afterward Marpa traveled to Nālandā, searching for and finally meeting Getsul Sherap Sengé. They went together to find Naropa at Riwo Sergyi Gönpa (Monastery of the Golden Mountain) in the city of Jong Metok Gyenpa (Land Adorned by Flowers). As soon as he met Naropa, Marpa placed the lama's feet on his head. Naropa responded:

My son, Marpa Lodrö, prophesied by the lama,
you are a suitable vessel who comes
from the Land of Snow in the north
to be my regent. It's good that you've arrived.

Naropa gave Marpa commentary on the root and the commentarial tantras of Hevajra along with the key instructions; he also bestowed the tantra of Cakrasaṃvara and others along with instructions on tummo; these were given so skillfully that Marpa penetrated their essential points.

Following Naropa's guidance, Marpa went to Lakshetra Monastery in the west and received from glorious Yeshé Nyingpo the empowerment of Guhyasamāja, its earlier and later root tantras, the lineage of commentary, and so forth—he was given everything.

On an island in the middle of a poisonous lake lived the master Kukuripa, a holder of the mother tantras. Naropa told Marpa to receive the tantra of Mahāmāyā from him, which he did. Kukuripa gave him the practice in its entirety—the tantra, the commentary, the sādhana in its long, middle, and short forms, and so forth—with nothing left out. When Marpa did the practice, he attained perfect yogic realization.

Afterward, Marpa traveled to Pullahari to meet Naropa, who told him, "I also received Mahāmāyā from Kukuripa, and he received Hevajra from me." Naropa gave Mahāmāyā to Marpa one more time, and the words were the same—none added or left out—and the meaning was also the same as before. The teachings of Naropa were clear and eloquent. Then, as Marpa had requested, Naropa gave him permission to study with the realized master Maitripa.

Marpa traveled to the cemetery known as Ri Metar Barwa (Mountain Blazing like Fire) where he met Maitripa. Marpa offered many full prostrations as well as supplications, which pleased Maitripa. He took Marpa as his disciple and gave him empowerments as well as the key instructions on mahāmudrā that illuminated Saraha's spiritual songs (*doha*). When Marpa put these into practice, a special realization arose, which he offered to Maitripa.

Then Naropa advised Marpa, "On the far side of a poisonous lake lives a wisdom ḍākiṇī. Go and ask her for The Four Seats. She has spoken clearly of many hidden yogis. Go to her and request key instructions." Thus Marpa departed, and through the power of blessings, he was able to cross the poisonous lake in an instant. He met the ḍākiṇī Chushingi Nyema, who gave him the empowerment of The Four Seats and others, completely satisfying Marpa.

After staying in India for twelve years, Marpa thought that he should return one time to Tibet and replenish his supply of gold. To express his great thanks, he arranged an excellent feast offering for Naropa and his disciples. Marpa sang a special song of realization, which included:

> This deluding samsara, the illusion of outer appearance,
> I've realized to be unborn mahāmudrā.
> This mental consciousness, the inner grasping one,
> just like meeting a dear old friend,
> mind knows to be its own true nature.

On his way back to Tibet, Marpa met Nyö Lotsāwa. Following Nyö's suggestion, Marpa gave the bundle of texts he had on his back to a yogi to carry. As they were crossing the Ganges, this yogi followed the devious orders of Nyö and, pretending that he had lost them, let Marpa's texts fall into the water. As soon as they had disembarked, Marpa seized the yogi and threatened to report him to the king. Continuing his ruse, Nyö said, "Oh, yes, one should do that," and gave various pieces of advice. After this, Marpa separated from Nyö and traveled on by himself.

When Marpa came to Nepal, Chitherpa and others welcomed him with gracious hospitality, but when Marpa came to Lhodrak, no one was there to greet him except for a teacher and a nun. They asked, "What Dharma do you know?"

Marpa replied, "I know Hevajra and Cakrasaṃvara, and others."

"We haven't heard of those," they replied and thought that he merely had a lot of knowledge.

However, the instant Ngoktön Chödor heard Marpa's name, he was filled with tremendous faith and went to find Marpa Lotsāwa. When they first met, Ngoktön Chödor offered Marpa his horse and all that it was carrying. Marpa said in jest:

> If this is a simple present, it's too much.
> If it's an offering for teachings, it's too little.

Ngoktön had come to request teachings on the great texts, and just as he wished, Marpa satisfied him with oral instructions. When Marpa went to the region of Phen, he gave Ngoktön empowerments. During this time Marpa met Marpa Golek, who became a disciple. Then Marpa took the considerable offerings he had been given and exchanged them for gold. With the thought that he must go to India soon, he returned to Lhodrak.

Marpa's fame and the power of his merit had greatly increased, and he gathered a large retinue and significant wealth. At this time he married the lady Dakmema and Chak Thungma. Darma Dodé was born as Dakmema's first son.

Then Marpa went alone to India, taking with him some eighty gold sang (about eighty ounces). When he met Chitherpa and Pentapa in Nepal, he offered them both a gift of gold. Later, in India, Marpa first received from Naropa the root tantra of Hevajra along with its commentarial tantra and key instructions.

Marpa then journeyed to see Maitripa and offered him gold as well. Marpa was able to cut through his doubts about the Dharma that he had already heard, and he newly received the empowerment of Guhyasamāja along with its commentary. He was also given the tantric text *A Drop of Mahāmudrā*, and he wrote out a copy. Continuing his travels, Marpa crossed over to the island in the poisonous lake and met again with the master Kukuripa, who was with the yoginī Rüpai Gyenchenma (Yoginī Adorned with Bones). Then Marpa rejoined Pal Yeshé Nyingpo and Singha Lingpa at Lakshetra in the west. Marpa offered gold to all of his lamas and received new tantras along with key instructions. He was also able to settle his questions about what he had received before. He copied and took with him the texts that he needed when he traveled to Pullahari to see Naropa. This time Naropa bestowed on him Indrabodhi's tradition of Cakrasaṃvara, the tantra of Buddha Kapala, and key instructions from a scroll in the tradition of Saraha. Marpa copied texts of the Dharma teachings he had previously received with such diligence that it was swiftly done.

When Marpa returned to Tibet, he was welcomed by Marpa Golek and others, who escorted him to his main seat in Lhodrak. Milarepa became his disciple and, to purify his karma, was made to build a nine-story tower (the famous Sekar Guthok) for Marpa's son. After Milarepa endured long hardship, Marpa finally gave him empowerments and instructions and sent him to meditate in Taknya Cave.

Marpa himself went north toward Central Tibet, and at Marpa Golek's place he gave empowerments. After the main practice, Marpa was thinking about the concluding rituals when he fell asleep for a short moment. Three ḍākiṇīs advised him that the pandita Naropa had departed for the Realm of Enjoying Space.

Meanwhile, as Milarepa was staying in Taknya Cave, a ḍākiṇī gave him prophetic advice: "You should ask for the teaching on transference of consciousness into another's body." When Milarepa told this to Marpa, he thought, "The time has come to receive these special instructions. Prompted by the ḍākiṇī, I must go to India, come what may. I can't miss making this connection." Since Marpa was well advanced in his years, everyone fervently pleaded with him not to go. But Marpa would not listen. "Now, whatever karma may come my way, I must go to India." So saying, he departed alone.

Marpa first arrived in Nepal and met with two Nepali brothers, also students of Naropa, who encouraged him: "Since you're a disciple who has kept samaya, you'll certainly meet Naropa. Make a feast offering and supplicate him." Afterward, Marpa went to Nālandā and met with Getsul Sherap Sengé, who told him, "You're too late. Last year, on the full moon after the New Year, Lord Naropa departed to the Realm of Enjoying Space. Why did you stay away for so long?"

"However, since you are a fortunate one," Getsul Sherap Sengé continued, "it's possible that you could still meet him. Make supplications." To begin with, Marpa made feast offerings for one month to Getsul Sherap Sengé and supplicated Naropa. Marpa then traveled to Bodh Gaya and all the other sacred sites, where he made offerings and prayers. Likewise, he supplicated Kukuripa, the ḍākiṇī Rūpai Gyenchenma, and the lord Maitripa while making offerings each month. Everyone predicted that Marpa would meet Naropa.

Marpa then went to see Riripa and Kasoripa, two Dharma brothers who were also sons of Naropa, who were staying in the same place. After Marpa had made offerings and supplicated them for a month, one predicted that Marpa would meet Naropa in eight months. For all that time, completely alone, Marpa searched for him in the cemetery groves. Then for seven days he supplicated Naropa with a single-pointed focus; suddenly Naropa stood clearly before him. Marpa threw his arms around Naropa and recited his litany of woes in searching for him.

Naropa said, "We shall proceed to Pullahari," and instantly they were there. Naropa gave Marpa the entire corpus of instructions: the practice of the six yogas that leads to full awakening in one lifetime; the whispered lineage of the ḍākiṇīs; the heart transmission of the fifteen cycles of instruction; the key instruction in a scroll; the completion-phase practice of nondual mind and prāṇa; teachings on the nature of mind that emphasized mahāmudrā; and the transference of consciousness into another body, a special part of The Four Seats.

When Marpa explained to Naropa how the prediction about the teaching of transference came from Milarepa (Thöpaga), Naropa sang his praises:

In the gloomy dark to the north
like the dazzling sun on snow
lives the noble Thöpaga.
To him I offer homage.

When Naropa placed his palms together and bowed his head, all the trees, grasses, and mountains leaned toward the north.

One time, at dawn when Marpa was sleeping, Naropa emanated into space a vivid and brilliant Hevajra mandala that displayed all nine deities, Hevajra's palace, and everything else to make the mandala complete.

"Son, wake up!" Naropa called, "the yidam Hevajra has come. To whom will you prostrate first? To the yidam deity or to me?"

"To the yidam deity," Marpa replied.

"All those figures you see now are my emanations," Naropa explained, and the deities dissolved into his heart.

"As a consequence of this circumstance, you will not have a family lineage. Your Dharma lineage, however, will last as long as the Buddha's teachings. If you and your son would strictly perform a long-life practice for three years without any difficulties, the obstacles to your family lineage could be averted. But you will not be able to complete it."

Placing his hand on Marpa's head, Naropa continued, "Son, I empower you as my regent to train disciples in the northern Land of Snow," and then Naropa sang spiritual songs. At the end, Naropa advised, "Go now to Central Tibet." He then rose higher and higher into the sky until he passed into the Realm of Enjoying Space.

After this meeting with Naropa, Marpa went to offer his final prostrations to Maitripa and his other teachers. All of them gave him very blessed objects to venerate and made aspiration prayers for him. When Marpa was in Bodh Gaya, he performed the transference of consciousness with the corpse of a rakshasa (a kind of female demoness) and became known as an undisputed master of meditation.

In brief, Marpa went three times to India and stayed there for twenty years in all. During these visits Marpa spent a total of sixteen years and seven months with Naropa. He perfected the complete key instructions from five masters: Naropa, Maitripa, Kukuripa, Yeshé Nyingpo, and the ḍākiṇī Rüpai Gyenchenma. In particular, Naropa and Maitripa empowered him as their representative to train disciples in the Land of Snow.

After Marpa returned to Tibet and was living in the Nine-Story Tower, he saw a hawk chase and strike a pigeon that died. Marpa performed the transference of consciousness into its body so that he himself looked like a corpse while the pigeon was flapping its wings and about to fly off. People nearby told the pigeon, "Stop that," so the bird passed away and the lama came back to life.

In order to avert the obstacles to his family lineage, Marpa and his son made the commitment to stay in retreat for three years. Marpa was living on the top floor of the Nine-Story Tower, and Darma Dodé on the one directly beneath him. Marpa gave his son all of the instructions, and Darma Dodé gained mastery over the transference of consciousness into another's body. At that time, Dakmema's wealthy older brother was on his way to a place where an annual fair was held. Not listening to Dakmema, Darma Dodé could not resist going. On the way back he fell off his horse and was dragged along the ground. When his skull cracked into eight parts and his brains spilled out, he departed from his body, and so Naropa's prediction came true.

A while later, Marpa examined his heart disciples to see what transmission and activity were most appropriate for each one. To Ngoktön of Shung he gave the root and commentarial transmission of Hevajra as well as the gradual methods and also the instructions on the blending and the transference of consciousness. To Tsurtön Wang Ngé from Döl he gave Guhyasamāja, the Five Stages, and the key instruction on transference. To Metön Chenpo from Tsangrong he gave Mahāmāyā and the instructions on the practice of radiant clarity. To Jetsun Milarepa he gave all the oral instructions and emphasized the practice of tummo. To Marpa Golek he gave the fifteen cycles of instruction of the heart lineage. Marpa gave key instructions and blessed objects for veneration to each of his other superior disciples, thus satisfying their hearts' desires.

Marpa's physical body dissolved into the expanse of all phenomena in the following way. When he had reached the venerable age of eighty-six, he gathered his disciples around him on the fifteenth (full-moon) day of the first month in the year of the Wood Female Ox (1085). He said, "Glorious Naropa has come to escort me with an assembly of ḍākiṇīs from the three places, and I must go. Prepare offerings and make aspiration prayers. As the practice of the transference of consciousness into another's body passes from one person to another, eventually even the name death will not exist."

"My lama told me, 'Go to the Realm of Enjoying Space where you can accomplish a greater benefit for beings.' Following his command, I'm going there."

Marpa entered into samādhi, and at that moment a white light dissolved into Dakmema. She was instantly transformed into white light that dissolved into the lama's heart. Right then, Marpa sat up straight and rested evenly in meditation. "My sons, if you meditate on transference, this is the way to do it." From the center of the Brahma aperture in the middle of his skull, with the sound of tsak! a triangular bone along with the hair flew six feet up into the space above Marpa. When it fell back to the ground, they could see inside the skull the five deities of Hevajra fashioned from the relic. Right then, a sphere of light the size of the moon exited from the opening in his skull into space. For seven days, rainbow lights filled the land of Lhodrak, flowers rained down, and the sounds of *damarus* and music were heard continuously.

Marpa had two lineages: the sons born into his family and the sons born through his Dharma. Born to Dakmema were the family lineage sons Darma Dodé and Darma Pal. Born to Chak Thungma were Darma Samten and others. The four great Dharma sons who delighted him were Ngoktön Chenpo, Tsurtön Wang Ngé, Metön Chenpo, and lord Milarepa. There were also the five sons who held his transmissions, the four with great devotion, and others. They all caused the teachings of the practice lineage to spread widely.

1. Lord Milarepa
2. Shönu Sangtsöl
3. Khyirawa Gönpo Dorjé
4. Rechungpa Dorjé Drakpa

Jetsun Milarepa

LORD OF YOGIS

1040–1123

> Son of the mountains, wearing a simple cloth in white,
> you limited food, clothes, and talk to the bare essentials
> and practiced correctly the instructions for method and liberation.
> Lord of Yogis, to you I pay homage.

On the twenty-fifth day of the seventh month in the year of the Iron Dragon, under the constellation Pusya (1040), Milarepa was born in the Korön area of Kya Ngatsa in Gungthang, located in the Mangyul district of Tibet. His father was Mila Sherap Gyaltsen, and his mother, Nyangtsa Kargyen. His father gave him the name Thöpaga (Joy to Hear), and when he was four, his mother gave birth to a sister named Peta Gön.

When Thöpaga was seven, his father fell gravely ill. Until the son was able to set up his own household, the father gave all of his wealth to his brother Yungdrung Gyaltsen and his wife Khyungtsé Paldren. Mila Sherap Gyaltsen entrusted his family and gave his Last Testament mainly to the aunt and uncle as well as to close and distant relatives, acquaintances, and dear friends: "When my son is able to establish a household and take Dzesé as his bride, you are to return to him all of this wealth, holding nothing back." With these words he passed away.

The uncle and aunt, however, seized all their wealth, so the mother and two children lost control. Moreover, the three were forced to work constantly to the point that the skin on their hands and feet split open. Their food and clothing were so wretched that they all grew pale and emaciated.

When Thöpaga turned fifteen, his mother prepared an abundant meal including meat and alcohol. She invited to her home (known as the Four Pillars and Eight Beams) the aunt and uncle plus her close relatives, good friends, neighbors, and local residents. She brought out her husband's Last Testament and made her request: "My son and Dzesé are ready to start their life together. It is time to return the wealth entrusted to you so that the son can take possession of his father's inheritance." Not only did the aunt and uncle stand firmly together in refusing to return the property, they also mercilessly beat the mother and children. "If the three of you have more supporters than we do," they said, "bring in your army. If you don't have enough people, try some sorcery," and they left.

Afterward, Thöpaga's mother sent him to a teacher from the older mantra tradition to learn reading. Once when Thöpaga went to a large gathering in lower Tsa where alcohol was served, he drank enough to become rather inebriated. On his way home, Thöpaga was captivated by the singers and began to sing himself. When his mother learned that it was her son carousing, she was aghast. Racing outside, she threw ashes in Thöpaga's face, and beat him on the head with her stick. She then collapsed, losing consciousness for a short while, and finally coming to, she began to wail. The mother and the two children sobbed together. Thöpaga promised his mother, "Whatever you want me to do, I'll do," so she sent him to learn how to cast spells.

Thöpaga traveled to Kyorpo Drong in Yarlung, where he met Lama Yungtön Trogyal. Thöpaga gave him all his gold and turquoise along with the offering of his body, speech, and mind, and then requested instruction in magic spells. The lama, however, sent him to study with Lama Yönten Gyatso in Nup Khulung, from whom Thöpaga received instructions and began to practice. One evening, after fourteen days, the signs of successful sorcery were clear. In the countryside of Kya Ngatsa, the eldest son of Thöpaga's uncle was getting married, and thirty-five people, including the uncle's sons and the bride, had gathered in their home to celebrate. At that time the house suddenly collapsed, killing all those inside, their corpses strewn over the churned up earth and debris.

Not satisfied with this, his mother sent a letter telling her son, "You should also send down a hailstorm." So Thöpaga went back the first lama, Yungtön Trogyal, to request instruction on conjuring hail. This time the lama agreed to teach him, and after a week the signs appeared. Thöpaga went to the region where the hail had descended and saw that it had filled up huge mountain ravines; in the fields it was so deep that the stalks of grain were not visible. His enemy had been vanquished.

Then a feeling of great remorse for his actions arose, and Thöpaga was directed to meet Marpa Lotsāwa, so he traveled to meet him and request Dharma teachings and instructions. In the beginning, Marpa made him perform sorcery and send a hailstorm, after which Marpa gave Thöpaga the name Thuchen, Great Sorcerer.

Marpa told him, "Now you should help to build the walls of a tower so my son Darma Dodé can move in. When you have finished, I will give you instructions. In the meantime I'll provide you with food and clothing." First, Marpa told him to build a round tower on a mountain ridge to the south. When Great Sorcerer was half finished, Marpa said, "The other day, I was not thinking very clearly. Destroy this tower and take the earth and stones back to where they came from." Great Sorcerer did exactly as instructed.

Marpa then told Great Sorcerer to build a tower shaped like a half moon on a mountain ridge to the west. When he was halfway done, Marpa made him destroy this as well. He then took Great Sorcerer to the peak of a mountain to the north and instructed him to build a triangular tower, which was known as a yogi's tower. Great Sorcerer began to build it, and when he was about one-third finished, Marpa again arrived and ordered him to demolish it. Great Sorcerer now had a huge sore on his back from carrying all the heavy loads. Finally Marpa gave him a reading transmission and an instruction on the common preliminaries and commented, "If you want oral instructions in the exceptional Secret Mantrayāna, you have to act in this way," and Marpa briefly related the story of the hardships and trials of Naropa. Great Sorcerer experienced such intense faith that tears welled forth.

Then Marpa said, "You must build a rectangular tower on the land held in common with my relatives. The tower must be nine stories high, with the tenth being a long spire. This will not be torn down, and when it is finished, I will give you instructions and provisions for retreat." While Great Sorcerer was building the foundation of the rectangular tower, Marpa's main disciples—Ngoktön Chödor of Shung, Dölgyi Tsurtön Wang Ngé of Döl, and Metön Tsönpo of Tsangrong—came by and playfully rolled a large stone into place as part of the foundation. Sometime later, Marpa arrived and said, "Take out that stone and carry it back to its original site." Great Sorcerer took apart the tower from the top down and carried the stone back to its place. Afterward Marpa said he should bring the stone back, so singlehandedly, the disciple lifted the stone, carried it to the tower, and placed it in the foundation. He continued working on the building until it was seven stories high, and a festering sore from carrying heavy loads appeared around his waist.

When Metön Tsönpo of Tsangrong came to request the Cakrasaṃvara empowerment, Great Sorcerer sat in the line of those to receive the initiation. Marpa asked him, "Great Sorcerer, if you have an offering for the empowerment, bring it here. If not, remove yourself from this line." He slapped him, grabbed him by the hair, and tossed him out.

The next morning the lama came and said, "Now for a little while, leave off building the remaining part of the tower. Instead construct at its base a covered walkway with twelve pillars. When you've finished, I'll give you empowerments and instructions." Having laid the foundations, Great Sorcerer began building the covered walkway. As it neared completion, Tsurtön Wang Ngé of Döl requested the Guhyasamāja empowerment from Marpa, and again Great Sorcerer sat in the row of those receiving it. Marpa asked, "What have you brought as an offering for the empowerment?" He scolded him, beat him with a shoe, and sent him out.

Great Sorcerer returned to his work on the covered walkway. Another sore opened on his back, and pus oozed from the three main lesions as his whole back became covered in wounds. The lama said, "Show me your sores," and he inspected them all. "Well, my lord Naropa experienced in his body twelve major and twelve minor trials, for a total of twenty-four. They all surpass yours. In my case, I served Naropa without regard for my life or resources. So if you yearn for the Dharma, work on the tower and don't get so swollen up with pride." Great Sorcerer shifted the basket for carrying mud to his front side and plastered the walls.

When Ngoktön Chödor and his followers came to request the Hevajra empowerment, Great Sorcerer offered a turquoise that Dakmema had given him, and he sat in the line of recipients. Marpa refused it as an offering, saying, "Great Sorcerer, if you yourself have something to offer, bring it here. If not, leave." The lama suddenly stood up and threw Great Sorcerer face down on the floor so that everything went dark. Marpa tossed him onto his back and the Great Sorcerer saw stars. When Marpa grabbed a stick, Great Sorcerer fled in terror, jumping out through a window. Overwhelmed with tremendous suffering, he thought of killing himself and wept.

Thinking that he could earn a salary as the servant of a wealthy person and have enough funds to request the Dharma, Great Sorcerer left without saying a word to Dakmema. On his way he was asked by an old man to read the *Prajñāpāramitā Sutra in Eight Thousand Verses*. There Great Sorcerer found the story of the Ever-Weeping One, who searched long and hard for his teacher. This gave Great Sorcerer the courage to return to Marpa, who said, "If your heart truly longs for the Dharma, construct three more stories for the tower. Then I'll give you instruction."

When Marpa was celebrating the tenth Tibetan day (dedicated to Guru Rinpoché) and making offerings, Dakmema again and again served up strong liquor to Marpa while his disciples also downed a few cups. They all became quite drunk and fell into a deep sleep. Dakmema slipped into the lama's residence, and took his seal, the ornaments of Naropa, and a ruby mala, all of which she wrapped in a fine cloth. She sealed a letter, making it resemble the lama's, gave everything to Great Sorcerer, and sent him off to request the Dharma from Lama Ngokpa. Great Sorcerer did receive teachings, but without Marpa's permission his practice did not bring any meditative experience.

Meanwhile the tower had been finished, and preparations were made for the son Darma Dodé's coming-of-age celebration and the consecration of the tower. Following his teacher's command, Lama Ngokpa had brought the Great Sorcerer along with him. Marpa severely scolded Lama Ngokpa: "For what reason under the sun did you ever give empowerments and oral instruction to that terrible person called Great Sorcerer?"

Great Sorcerer thought, "In this body, I'm not receiving the Dharma, and further, I'm doing a lot of negative things." As he was preparing to kill himself, Marpa sent for him and made him the main guest, saying, "As a way to purify his negative actions, I have tormented the Great Sorcerer with suffering. If the work on the tower had been done for my own benefit, it would have been enough to direct him in a peaceful way. If I had been able to put this faithful son of mine through nine great torments, he would have become a buddha without any aggregates remaining and would have had no need to take rebirth again. This didn't happen, so there remains some small negativity thanks to all of Dakmema's fussing.

"Nevertheless, his major negativities have been eliminated through eight great torments and many minor ones. Now I shall accept him as my disciple and give him all the oral instructions, which are like this old man's heart. I'll also give him whatever he needs for retreat and put him into meditation. Now be happy!"

That evening, Great Sorcerer's head was shaved, his clothes were changed, and he was given the name Mila Dorjé Gyaltsen (Mila Vajra Victory Banner). Marpa gave him the common lay precepts belonging to the vows of individual liberation and also the bodhisattva vow. The following day, Marpa bestowed a ripening empowerment from the Secret Mantra.

When Marpa was revealing the mandala of Cakrasaṃvara, Milarepa vividly saw in the sky the deity Cakrasaṃvara surrounded by ḍākiṇīs and ḍākas. At this time, he was given the secret name of Pal Shepa Dorjé (Glorious Laughing Vajra).

Marpa then sent Milarepa to meditate in Taknya Cave. While he was practicing, Milarepa placed a burning lamp full of oil on his head and did not move until it was empty. Thus he meditated day and night. After eleven months had passed, Dakmema broke down the wall to his cave. He came out and related in detail to Marpa and her how an understanding of his experience and realization had arisen.

Early one morning, in a state of radiant clarity, Marpa saw his main heart sons and knew what their particular Dharma transmissions and activities would be. He gave Milarepa the oral instructions on tummo (the yoga of heat), as well as the hat of Maitripa and clothes of Naropa, and advised him: "Wander through the mountains of snow and slate while practicing view and meditation." Initially he counseled Milarepa to remain nearby for a few years, so he meditated in Sangphuk. In the presence of his lama, Milarepa developed the first seedlings of experience and realization.

After a while Milarepa had powerful memories of his mother and appealed to Marpa for permission to return home just once. Marpa replied, "You may return to your country, but it will be difficult to meet your mother. If you wish to go, I'll give you leave. The two of us, father and son, will not meet again in this life. Because of you, the teachings of the Buddha, and in particular the Karma Kagyü, will spread." Marpa fully transmitted to Milarepa the ḍākiṇī's oral instructions, which are given to only one person and not revealed to others.

After a few days Marpa advised Milarepa, "Spend your time in all the different types of mountains, covered in snow, slate, or forests, and raise the victory banner of practice. If you can practice, that is serving your lama. It is repaying the kindness of your parents and benefiting living beings—these all are practice in itself. Do not remain longer than seven days in one place. Make staying in mountain retreats your whole life. This is benefiting yourself and others."

Having offered his final prostrations to Marpa and Dakmema, Milarepa placed their feet on his head and finally departed for his home. When he arrived, Milarepa found his house, once like a temple, in a state of collapse, and he discovered his mother's pale bones inside. Overwhelmed with grief, he knew deeply that samsara has no essence. After making small offering figurines of the bones, Milarepa turned to his yidam deity practice. Behind his house there was an excellent cave, and he stayed there in meditation.

Then, without anyone knowing, Milarepa left for Drakar Taso Cave (White Rock, Horse Tooth Cave) where he remained for over three years, alone and happy, meditating day and night as his practice developed. When his food ran out, he ate nettles and continued meditating. Since he had no clothes for his outside and no roasted barley or nutritious food for his inside, Milarepa's body became a skeleton while all the skin and hair on his body turned a green hue.

After meditating intensely for several years, he found that during the day he could manifest miracles, such as changing his body into whatever shape he wished. During the night, when he dreamed, he could manifest hundreds of emanations of his mind and body, each one of which went to the pure realm of a buddha and received teachings. Milarepa revealed inconceivable miracles. Meditating with his mind in a state of great delight, he was actually able to fly in the sky. He would fly to Minkyuk Dripmai Dzong to meditate and then fly to Drakar Taso to practice.

Milarepa thought, "If I am to help living beings, I should do something now to benefit others." His yidam deity replied, "In this life you should focus on fulfilling the command of your lama. There's nothing greater you could do to serve the Buddha's teachings and to benefit others." Certain that it would bring great benefit to the teachings and living beings, Milarepa determined to devote himself to practice. So he passed his entire life this way, becoming a supreme example of practicing Dharma and inspiring fortunate people in the future to give up their worldly life and to engage in practice.

True to his resolution, Milarepa meditated in remote places that are now famed as his fortresses: the six outer, the six inner, and the six secret fortresses plus two more, as well as the four great caves that were famous and the four that were not. In these locations, he placed his disciples on the path of ripening and liberation. Among his human disciples, there were twenty-five who attained realization:

his eight heart sons, among whom were the sun-like disciple Gampopa and the moon-like disciple Rechungpa; another thirteen who were very close; and the four Dharma sisters. The number of nonhuman disciples Milarepa trained is beyond number. More about all of them can be found in the *One Hundred Thousand Songs of Milarepa*.

At the end of his life, when Milarepa had completed all of his vast activities, the geshé Tsakphupa persuaded a woman to slip poison into the yogurt she would offer Milarepa. After accepting it, Milarepa appeared to become extremely ill. In a show of false concern, the geshé said to him, "Please transfer your illness to me." First, Milarepa transferred the sickness to a door, and then to the geshé, who fainted from the unbearable pain and almost died. Milarepa took back most of the illness, and the geshé, filled with intense regret, made a complete confession. Later he became someone who took delight in the Dharma.

When Milarepa spoke of his Last Testament, he said: "The main part of my Last Testament is about the gold that I have accumulated throughout my life. There is also a letter on how to divide this among my disciples. You'll find the gold buried underneath this hearth. After I've died, look here and do as the letter says."

At the age of eighty-four, in the Tibetan year of the Water Hare (1123), on the fourteenth day of the last winter month as the sun rose in brilliance, Milarepa dissolved his physical form into the expanse of all phenomena. After six days, the disciples examined the corpse and found that it had become the size of an eight-year-old boy, whose radiant face shone like a yidam deity's.

Before Rechungpa arrived they had tried to burn the corpse, but it would not catch fire. When Rechungpa came, he offered a heartrending sevenfold lament during which the corpse lost its radiance and burst into flames. Though Milarepa had already dissolved into luminosity, he rose again, sitting in half-lotus with his right hand in the teaching mudra reaching down to suppress the flames and his left hand supporting his cheek. He spoke to his disciples, "Listen to this old man's final words," and Milarepa sung his final song, "The Six Essential Points." The last verses counsel:

> Supplicate as one
> the lamas, yidams, and dākiṇīs.
> Practice as one
> view, meditation, and conduct.
> Blend into one
> this life, the next, and the bardo in between.
>
> This is the last of all instruction.
> This is the end of my final words.
> There's nothing but this, Rechungpa.
> Bring it into your experience, my son.

Milarepa then dissolved back into radiant clarity.

Following Milarepa's Last Testament, the main disciples dug underneath the hearth and looked inside. They found a small knife, a lump of brown sugar, and a letter, all of it rolled up in a square of the finest Benares muslin. They unrolled the letter to read Milarepa's words:

> With the small knife you should cut the lump of sugar and the muslin, which will never run out. Cut and give them to as many people as possible. Whoever tastes the sugar or touches the cloth will be liberated

> from the lower realms, for these are the food and clothing of my meditation, and they have also been blessed by the Victorious Ones of the past. Whoever hears my name just once and has faith will not be born in the lower realms for seven lifetimes and will recall their previous life in their next seven lives. This follows the prophecy of the Victors from the past. And if anyone says that Milarepa collected gold, stuff their mouth with shit.

Though the older disciples were steeped in sorrow, this made them all laugh.

They used the knife to cut the sugar into innumerable pieces, and each piece became the same size as the original. Similarly, no matter how much they sliced the cloth, each square equaled the original. These pieces of cloth and sugar were then given out to others. When the sick and miserable came in touch with these, their suffering disappeared. The ill-willed and those afflicted with negative thoughts or actions were transformed so that their faith, diligence, deeper knowing, and compassion increased. The sugar and cloth lasted the whole lifetime of each recipient.

1. Lord Gampopa
2. Śākyamuni Buddha
3. Gomchung Sherap Jangchup
4. Gompa Tsultrim Nyingpo
5. Barompa Darma Wangchuk
6. Phakmo Drupa Dorjé Gyalpo
7. Lhola Yakpa Jangchup Ngödrup

Gampopa

LORD OF DHARMA

1079–1153

You came to Tibet just as the Buddha foretold
in the *White Lotus of Compassion Sutra*.
I bow to Gampopa whose instructions integrated
the teachings of the Kadampa, mahāmudrā, and the six yogas.

Countless eons ago, the Bhagavan, the Tathāgata, was present in this world as the noble king Utterly Pure Moon of the Precious Lotus, and Gampopa was the bodhisattva Metok Dazé (Beautiful Moon Flower). Through benefiting numerous people by offering his life to eliminate their suffering, he was able to mature and liberate myriads of bodhisattvas and living beings.

Gampopa said in the famous song "Hallo! Come Back Up":

In the presence of the Lord, the perfect Buddha,
the Bhagavan and protector Śākyamuni,
when I was Youthful Moonlight, I requested
the *King of Samādhi Sutra* and the Buddha gave it.

When Śākyamuni Buddha was teaching the *King of Samādhi Sutra*, Gampopa was the central figure in his retinue of bodhisattvas and known as Candraprabha Kumāra (Youthful Moonlight). At that time he made the commitment to spread the teachings of this sutra. Further, in the *White Lotus of Compassion Sutra*, the Buddha stated:

> Ānanda, after I have passed away, at a future time in the region to the north, there will come one named the Monk Physician. He has engaged in extraordinary activity for a past king and served and honored hundreds of thousands of buddhas. He created the roots of goodness and brought forth the highest intention. To benefit many people and bring them joy, he correctly entered the Mahāyāna path. Further, he has upheld the collected scriptures on a bodhisattva's path, praised the Mahāyāna, and taught it perfectly.

Marpa Lotsāwa foretold the coming of Gampopa and his disciples when he interpreted Milarepa's dream, in which the vulture represents Milarepa and the single chick, Gampopa:

> The vulture giving birth to a single chick
> shows that one beyond compare will come.
> Better than this disciple will be his students,
> coming in a great crowd, each one better than the last.

Gampopa was born in Bönyi, located in Central Tibet's Nyal area. His clan was also Bönyi, one of three clans with the name Nyi (the others being Gyanyi and

Yunyi). His father was King Ga of Nya, and his mother, Lady Shomo Sangché. The middle of three sons, Gampopa was born in 1079, the year of the Earth Female Sheep, amid many wondrous signs. He received the name Darma Drak (Fame of the Dharma).

Over the years he became skilled in medicine and mantra, and he married the sister of a local leader known as Dharma Ö (Light of the Dharma). The couple had a son and daughter, both of whom died. Then Gampopa's wife became gravely ill, and as she was passing away, she implored him, "Practice pure Dharma." With all of his suffering, Gampopa became thoroughly weary of samsara and departed for Dakpo. At the age of twenty-six he took full ordination along with the lay precepts and novice vows, receiving them all from the Mangyul Geshé Loden Sherap and the master Shapa Lingpa. He was given the name Sönam Rinchen (Precious Merit). With this master Shapa Lingpa, Gampopa studied numerous key instructions from the tantras, including the father and mother tantras.

Later, Gampopa heard that Lama Jangchup had a copy of Milarepa's oral instructions. After he received them, Gampopa experienced excellent calm abiding and stayed in samādhi for thirteen days. Sangkar Lotsāwa taught him yoga tantra and Cakrasaṃvara. Studying with Ja Dulzin, Gampopa developed into an expert on the Vinaya texts.

Gampopa then went to Üru in the north and studied for seven months, training in the stages of the path with the Kadampa Nyukrumpa. An utterly pure relative bodhicitta was born in Gampopa's mind, and he said that from that day forth, he was never separated from it. Afterward, for another seven months in Chakri Gongkha, Gampopa studied numerous key instructions with Geshé Chakriwa Dawa. He also received teachings on the protector Drikukma and saw him face to face. Wishing to develop further, Gampopa went to see the geshé Gyayön Dak, with whom he studied all the key instructions of Atiśa. In his meditation Gampopa focused on practices of the gradual path, and his previous experience of bliss and clarity diminished slightly while weariness and revulsion came to predominate.

Thinking, "Now I really need to practice," Gampopa built a dwelling, and by practicing he was able to restore his previous meditative concentration and maintain it. He had only a short daily period of sleep, and in his dreams he saw numerous amazing signs, which are explained in the *Genuine Light of Gold* and *The Sutra of the Ten Bodhisattva Levels*. During this time he did not eat for many days but felt no hunger. His body was continuously filled with the meditative experience of bliss.

One time, Gampopa rose from his meditation to refresh himself, and he heard three old beggars lamenting. One said, "The likes of us don't have much merit. If each of us could just get a heap of roasted barley mixed with butter and some cooked vegetables, we'd have our food taken care of." Another said, "That might be what you wish for. I really want to be like the king Tsedé." The third one said, "Death will also come to the king Tsedé. When that happens, nothing will help. What I'd like is to resemble Milarepa, Lord of Yogis. He doesn't need clothes, and his food is the wisdom ambrosia provided by ḍākiṇīs. He rides lions, flies through the air, and has no fear of death." The moment Lord Gampopa heard about Milarepa, tremendous faith filled him with such a sudden force that his hair stood on end and tears welled up in his eyes. A long time passed without him knowing it.

It turned out that these beggars were staying at a guesthouse not far away. When he found them, Gampopa asked about Milarepa. One of them responded, "The one called Milarepa is a disciple of Marpa Lotsāwa, and his teachings are said to be on the six yogas of Naropa. I haven't seen Milarepa myself. Most people who go to meet him don't find him. Some see a crystal stupa, some see the Buddha. He has many manifestations. For the most part he just stays in the mountains of Drin and Nyenam."

"If I go there, how about coming along with me?" Gampopa asked. "You're young. I couldn't keep up with you," the beggar replied. "But if you go yourself, you'll find him. He's very famous."

Then Gampopa delighted the three beggars with an abundant meal of roasted barley and vegetable stew. The next morning he looked for them but couldn't discover where they had gone. He was convinced that they were not actual beggars but the lama's emanations sent to inspire him. Filled with an overwhelming faith, he decided to leave. Gampopa supplicated the lama inseparable from the Three Jewels and fell asleep to dream about blowing a long *radung* horn whose sound filled the whole universe—nothing was more powerful.

Gampopa sold a good piece of land for gold and tea, and went to ask leave from Geshé Chakriwa, who said, "If you've come looking for teachings on the Secret Mantra, I have them." Though Gampopa made his request three times, this teacher did not allow him to leave, so Gampopa went to another, who said, "Do as you please." When Gampopa asked Geshé Yöndak, he replied: "Stay no more than a year. This yogi is certainly a realized master. Inquire about every aspect of Dharma and request his entire oral instructions. Then bring back the gift of Dharma." Another, Chen Ngawa, advised, "If by all means you must go, then do not change the Kadampa robes you are wearing." Geshé Nyukrumpa told him, "Do not forget this old man." Gampopa was delighted to have received these lamas' permission, and, turning his mind toward Jetsun Milarepa, he departed.

Around this time, Jetsun Milarepa's cotton-clad yogis asked him, "Please appoint someone to hold your seat and lineage." Milarepa replied, "My lineage holder will come soon. Known as the Physician, he's a fully ordained monk following the

Vinaya. Last night, I dreamt that I held in my hands a crystal vase filled with amrita. A fully ordained monk from Central Tibet carried a silver vase into which my amrita poured like falling rain until the silver vase was brim full. My lineage will be carried by a monk, not a cotton-clad yogi."

At a day and a half's journey from Milarepa, Gampopa came down with an illness that gave him severe headaches, made him dizzy, and unbalanced his prāṇa, so he fainted again and again. Praying fervently to Milarepa, he was cured. Milarepa was teaching during this time; sometimes he would smile, and other times he would shed glistening tears. When asked why, he replied: "My son, Üpa Tönpa (the Teacher from Central Tibet) is coming here, so I'm happy and smiling. Since he is repeatedly collapsing at resting places by the roadside, I feel compassion for him. He'll be arriving soon, and whoever guides him here will not fall into the lower realms."

As he traveled, Gampopa came to Drodé Tashi Gang, where he found a woman weaving and asked her, "Where does the lord of yogis Milarepa stay?" It turned out that Gampopa had come across a female disciple of Milarepa who had the information he needed. Respectfully she replied: "You won't be able to get there tonight. Stay here in the upper part of my house. Yesterday," she related, "when I was in the presence of Milarepa, he said that there would be a teacher coming from Central Tibet. If we would guide this teacher to him, we wouldn't have to fear rebirth in the lower realms. So if my daughter, who's a meditator, went with you, that would mean she was the guide."

With some pride Gampopa thought, "The lama knows I'm coming and has given a prophecy. I'm a suitable vessel, so I'll receive oral instructions without any difficulty." Milarepa knew this and did not receive Gampopa for two weeks. Finally, at the age of thirty-one, Gampopa met Milarepa, who was sitting on top of a large boulder. Gampopa was going to offer him four measures of gold and a brick of tea, but Sewen Repa told him, "Just come into Milarepa's presence. There's no difference between offering him gold and piling it in front of an animal. Come with empty hands."

When Gampopa made his offerings, Milarepa said, "Gold and this old man's mind don't agree. And I have no stove to boil up tea. Keep these things as provisions for your practice."

Gampopa replied, "I've come from far away and implore you to care for me with compassion."

"You haven't come all that far. People arrive here from as far away as Eastern Tibet and India. What's your name?"

"Sönam Rinchen."

Milarepa repeated "Sönam Rinchen" three times and commented, "Sönam (merit) comes from gathering a great accumulation, and Rinchen (precious) means precious for all six types of beings." He filled a skull cup with alcohol and gave it to Gampopa, saying, "Drink this." Since Gampopa was a fully ordained monk and many people were present, he hesitated, unable to accept it. "Don't think about it so much and just drink," Milarepa advised, so Gampopa drank it to the last drop. This created the auspicious connection to hold Milarepa's lineage and receive the complete oral instructions.

On the basis of a sindhura mandala, Milarepa bestowed empowerments full of blessing. He asked Gampopa about the empowerments he had already received and about the samādhis he had experienced. Milarepa commented, "You have a high attainment, but it's that of a god on the level of no-perception."

Then Gampopa asked Milarepa, "Do the Kadampas also have many teachings on the Secret Mantrayāna?"

"They belong to the Secret Mantrayāna, but they don't have the key instructions," he replied.

"What is the main method for gathering merit?" asked Gampopa. Milarepa responded, "Greater than the merit gained by making offerings to all the buddhas of the three times is making offerings to a single pore of the lama. Better even than that is not wasting the lama's oral instructions and putting them into practice. That is the greatest merit."

"Is it possible to attain full awakening in one lifetime?"

"For one who doesn't care a feather for this life, who receives an authentic lama's oral instructions and continuously practices them, if they are superior, they'll be liberated in this very life; if they are middling, at death or in the bardo; and if inferior, in seven or sixteen lives.

"You should not go along with those who merely talk about the Dharma. Attune your mind to those who practice meditation and listen to their words. The most profound advice of all is to follow the renunciates who have given up attachment to this life. Be like them. Those who focus merely on this existence use it to study the eight worldly concerns."

Milarepa continued: "If you do not cut through what mind takes for its basis, then no matter how good your experiences of bliss, clarity, and nonthought might be, they do not transcend the three realms. This is called meditative experience without cutting through the root.

"What is the correct path? An authentic lama guides a disciple who is a proper vessel. Through a variety of methods, the lama indicates the natural mind present in all living beings. After this has been pointed out, disciples naturally realize the view though meditation: afflictions cease by themselves, concepts are released into their ground, and primordial wisdom manifests.

"The experience of resting in the abiding nature cannot be put into words or shown by any form of expression. It is ineffable, just like the bliss of a young maiden or the dream of a mute. This fundamental nature is present in everyone, but they do not know it.

"So it is important to rely on a lama who holds a lineage. Natural or ordinary mind does not rely on any foundation, however profound it may be. This mind cannot be illustrated by analogy or realized through any form of expression—no verbal convention can touch it. So don't try to capture and manipulate it. Rest relaxed in a fresh state without any particular aim."

Gampopa thought, "I've had this opportunity to meet such a great lama. I should stay for a long time and serve him. Having penetrated his oral instructions, without fail I should engage in practice right up to the very end." Following his lama's instruction, Gampopa went out to beg for alms in Drin and Nyenam, and that evening he entered Drodé Phuk (Cave of Joy and Delight), where he engaged with great diligence in spiritual practice.

After Milarepa gave Gampopa instructions on inner heat (*tummo*), he wore only cotton cloth when meditating, and a blissful warmth naturally radiated. After seven days, Gampopa directly saw the buddhas of the five families. When he told this to Milarepa, he replied, "That's no different from pressing your eyeballs and seeing two moons. There's a little grasping at the winds of the five elements. It's neither a fault nor a positive quality."

Gampopa went back to his meditation with enthusiasm. In three months, he saw at dawn the billion-fold world as a huge spinning wheel, and he lost consciousness. When he asked Milarepa about this, he replied, "The winds of the right (*rasanā*) and left (*lalanā*) channels entered into the central one (*avadhūti*)."

When signs like these happen, showing that consciousness has ceased, if one grasps at them, that apprehension can become an obstacle to higher levels of the path. Therefore, Milarepa said that they were neither a fault nor a positive quality. When Gampopa told him about his sixteen wondrous dreams, such as sitting in full lotus on a golden flower, Milarepa simply responded with a song.

Before a month was over, Gampopa had visions of the Medicine Buddha and his seven brothers, the infinite sambhogakāya realms, and the deeds of the thousand buddhas, in particular Buddha Śākyamuni. When Gampopa related this to Milarepa, he said, "Now you've looked at the face of the yidam deity. You've seen both the sambhogakāya and the nirmāṇakāya manifest. You have yet to meet the dharmakāya. At this point, you don't need to stay with me. Go to Central Tibet and meditate there. If modes of higher perception develop, it's important to keep them secret."

Milarepa continued, "Son, the realization that sees the unfabricated nature of the mind has dawned for you. Further, you are filled with a devotion that sees this old man as an actual buddha. Basing yourself on this realization, continue gathering the accumulations. To the east of here is a mountain known as Gampo Dar where disciples who are suitable vessels will come. Go there and benefit living beings. Your name is Gelong Dorjé Dzinpa Chenpo Dzamling Drakpa (Fully Ordained Monk Holding the Great Vajra, Famous Throughout the World).

Milarepa gave Gampopa all of his empowerments and blessings, plus his complete teachings with nothing left out. When Milarepa placed a great torma on Gampopa's head, the ḍākiṇīs and protectors empowered him. Milarepa foretold, "Son, you will benefit immeasurable numbers of living beings. And finally, my son, come back to the mountains of Drin and Nyenam on the fourteenth of the first (horse) month in the year of the Male Hare." Gampopa stayed with Milarepa for thirteen months, and at the age of thirty-two he traveled to Central Tibet.

Milarepa said to his cotton-clad yogis, "Last night I dreamt that a great vulture flew from nearby me to Central Tibet and landed on the peak of a tall mountain where an incalculable number of swans had gathered. I wondered why the vulture had stayed a short time and then flown away. Then I saw that each swan was surrounded by some five hundred swans who were their attendants. The region was filled to the brim with golden swans. This Üpa Tönpa (Teacher from Central Tibet) will come to benefit living beings beyond number. I am a yogi, but in the future there will be many monks."

After staying with Milarepa, Gampopa received teachings on White Tārā from the Kadampa geshé Nyukrumpa, and engaging in her practice extended Gampopa's life. When Gampopa heard that on the fourteenth day of the first month of the Male Hare year (the day he was supposed to return) Milarepa had passed away, he lost consciousness for a short while. While Gampopa had stayed with a group of Kadampas, the meditative experience he had developed under Milarepa weakened. He now recalled his lama's words and fervently prayed to Milarepa. Gampopa thought, "Like connecting with an old friend, I met the fundamental nature of mind, and the realization of mahāmudrā appeared vast like the sky. Previously, I perceived the Lord of Yogis as a greatly realized master, and now I know that he is actually a buddha." Thinking of him, Gampopa felt boundless devotion.

Ödé Güngyal, the local protector of the place where Gampopa stayed, had received refuge and bodhisattva vows from Gampopa. The protector said to him, "My son will engage in beneficial activity at Daklha Gampo. Please come to stay there." So in his forties, Gampopa went to Daklha. He thought of staying in a sealed retreat for twelve years and built a place for that purpose in Sanglung. When he felt that it was time to enter retreat, a woman appeared holding peacock feathers in her hand, her body smeared with ashes. She advised him, "Rather than staying in a sealed retreat for twelve years, it's better that you use this time to spread the teachings."

Soon after this, crowds of worthy disciples from Central, Western, and Eastern Tibet gathered around Gampopa. It was not long before they all perfected the qualities of the channels, winds, and drops and developed the six modes of higher perception. Disciples had the qualities that came from training in the proper, upright sitting posture and remaining a long time. Keeping silence, they passed all their time in strict mountain retreats or in sealed retreats.

Finally, the time came when Gampopa said, "I won't be staying in this world for much longer. Those of you who have Dharma teachings to request or questions to ask should do so soon." He continued, "You all might be thinking, 'People in the future will not be able to meet him.' However, I have written texts, such as the *Ornament of Precious Liberation* and the *Precious Garland of the Supreme Path*. Studying them is no different from meeting me." At the end, he sat straight up and looked clearly into space, saying, "Free of thought, I see everything vividly." He rested evenly in the abiding nature without elaboration, and as the sun reached halfway down the mountain, he withdrew his nirmāṇakāya into the space of all phenomena. It was the fifteenth day of the eighth month in the year of the Water Female Bird (1153) when he was seventy-five years old. Rainbows shone throughout the sky, and booming sounds like the thundering of celestial drums resounded everywhere. The sky in front of his monastery at Gampo was radiant with one hundred and eight crystal stupas shedding their brilliant light.

Gampopa's remains were placed on a jeweled throne, and a great variety of offerings were beautifully arranged. Two young monks were given the role of caretaking the offerings, and they naturally developed mahāmudrā meditation. All the great practitioners came out of retreat and stayed near the throne making prayers. For three days they remained in a special meditative experience of samādhi; they had absolutely no inclination to sleep or torpor and no desire to eat or drink.

When Gampopa's remains were placed in the fire, it did not affect his heart. Further, when his heart was placed in a pan and burnt with charcoal, its shape became even clearer. The master Gompa said, "This relic has come to us as a sign of being held by his compassion." After Gampopa's heart was bathed with perfumed water, it was displayed to the great meditators and they received empowerment from it.

Gampopa's foremost disciples were Dakpo Gomtsul, who held the main seat of Gampo, and the three men from Eastern Tibet: the First Karmapa Düsum Khyenpa, Phakmo Drupa, and Saltong Shogom. There were also Barompa Darma Wangchuk, Gomchung, and a host of others.

Part Two

The Illustrated Lives of the Seventeen Karmapas

Introduction

This section presents the spiritual biographies of the successive incarnations in the Golden Garland of the Lords of Dharma, the Gyalwang Karmapas, who have been predicted in many texts. The *Root Tantra of Mañjuśrī* states:

> Having a name with *ka* at the beginning and *ma* at the end,
> a noble being will come and clarify the teachings.

A golden scroll from Lama Shang's *Terma of the Steep Gorge Rock* reveals:

> The lama who is Düsum Khyenpa
> has the name Dharmakīrti.
> After the teachings of the Buddha Maitreya,
> he will be known as the Lion Buddha
> and will spread the teachings widely.
> This one is Dharmakīrti himself.

In this way, referring to the Karmapa as Dharmakīrti—the name he was given when he took a renunciate's vow—Lama Shang foretold the coming of the Karmapa as the Sixth Buddha, the Lion's Roar, in the form of a bodhisattva who will be an extraordinary leader to guide disciples through these degenerate times. Śākyaśrī also gave a similar prophecy.

In the *Treasury of Knowledge*, Jamgön Kongtrul quotes Machik Lapdrön (1055–1149/53), who stated that as long as the teachings of the Buddha Śākyamuni last, we will not see individuals as great as the Gyalwang Karmapa and the lord Tsongkhapa.

Guru Rinpoché, the second Buddha, also predicted many times that inseparable from him, there will continuously appear (sometimes clearly known and sometimes not) in this very Land of Snow, a great being who is a vajra master bearing the name of the One Who Holds the Black Crown. All who see, hear, recall, or touch him will not experience the lower realms and will enter the path that leads to liberation and the higher realms.

In the terma scripture of lord Nyang (Nyangral Nyima Özer, 1124–92), it is said:

> Avalokiteśvara, the Great Compassionate One,
> appears as the one named Karmapa
> so that China, Tibet, and Mongolia may be tamed.
> With the activity of Jinasāgara,
> residing at Tsurphu, he is Düsum Khyenpa.

The great tertön Sangyé Lingpa made similar predictions. Another noble being predicted in the sutras was the lord Milarepa's heart son Gampopa, who was like the sun and famed as the Monk Physician, the Peerless Doctor from Dakpo. He was clearly foretold in the *King of Samādhi Sutra* and other texts. His main heart sons were the four elders of the Kagyü; from among these four crown jewels of the lineage, the Karmapa is the holder of the teachings of the Kamtsang Kagyü.

In general, the name *karma* means "action" or "activity," and the syllable *pa* means "the holder of" or "the master of." Since he is the one who performs the activity of all the buddhas of the three times, he is famous as the Karmapa. His name can also have the meaning of "the one empowered to perform the activity of all the buddhas" or can be interpreted to mean "the one who wears the Black Crown." While the First Karmapa Düsum Khyenpa was taking the renunciate's vows and a tuft of hair on his crown was being cut, wisdom dākiṇīs and Cakrasaṃvara with his assembly of yidam deities placed on the Karmapa's head the Black Crown, which was woven from the hair of dākiṇīs. At that time he was given the name Karmapa as the one who performs the activity of all the buddhas.

Afterward, in harmony with the auspicious connection between the vision of the Black Crown and the cutting of his hair, the Karmapa would wear the Black Crown, which became very famous. There are also stories of a few disciples with purified karma who have seen the Black Crown naturally resting on the Karmapa's head, even though he was not wearing it.

The Karmapa is also known as the first tulku (reincarnate lama) in Tibet. The Third Karmapa Rangjung Dorjé was born in 1284. When he was three years old, he talked about memories of his previous lives just as if he were the Karmapa. After he identified the Black Hat and a specific text belonging to his previous incarnation, the tradition began of empowering the Karmapa on a golden throne as the reincarnation of his predecessor. It is widely known that previous to the Karmapa, there was no tradition of recognizing tulkus in Tibet.

As he is described above, the one renowned as the Karmapa is the very embodiment of the activity of the buddhas from all three times; a great being of uncountable qualities; an immense treasure of loving-kindness free of any reference point; one who can change our impure, ordinary appearances just by seeing him or hearing his voice. He is the one who gives great liberation upon seeing, great liberation upon hearing, and great liberation upon remembering. For all lifetimes, he is the ultimate protector, unerring and supreme.

1. The First Karmapa Düsum Khyenpa
2. Palchen Galo
3. Lama Berotsana
4. Kyopa Jikten Sumgyi Gönpo
5. Taklung Thangpa Tashipal
6. Tsangpa Gyaré Yeshé Dorjé
7. Attendant Namkha Ö
8. Gönpo Chakshipa

The First Karmapa Düsum Khyenpa

1110–93

Düsum Khyenpa was born in Ratak, located in Treshö, a countryside surrounded by snow mountains in an eastern area of the Amdo region near Kham. His father was the tantric practitioner Dorjé Gön, and his mother was named Gangcham. He took birth in 1110 according to the Western calendar; in the Tibetan system, it was during the second sixty-year cycle in the year of the Iron Male Tiger. He was given the name Gephel (Increasing Virtue).

From his grandfather Gompa Tongpön Sherap Gönpo and from his father, he received the practice of Lhamo Rangjungma (The Naturally Arising Goddess, a form of Palden Lhamo) as well as a few teachings of the Nyingma tradition. At the age of eleven, he accomplished the practice of Palden Lhamo, had a clear vision of her, and left his footprint in a rock. Later, in the village of Duru, an adversary of his was killed by the kick of a horse, and this gave Gephel the reputation of possessing great powers. He also received much excellent advice from Lama Berotsana Vajra and Palzin.

When he was sixteen in 1125, at the Kadampa monastery known as Treka Drak, he took monastic vows with Khenpo Chogi Lama and Chak Sengé Drak acting as preceptors, and was given the name Pal Chökyi Drak (Glorious Fame of the Dharma). For two years, he served the abbot and participated in the work of the

Sangha. Familiar with the past, he spoke at length about what had previously occurred. In harmony with the way things are, he could state that in the present world, this or that emanation was now benefiting living beings. Knowing directly what would happen in the future, he was able to make prophecies that turned out just as he had foretold. Therefore, although his actual name was Chökyi Drakpa, he was known as Düsum Khyenpa (Knower of the Three Times).

At the age of twenty, with Gya Marwa and Geshé Chapa Chöseng, he studied the Madhyamaka-Svātantrika texts of Śāntarakṣita, Kamalaśīla, and Jñānagarbha as well as the five Dharmas of Maitreya. Then he studied the Collection of Five Madhyamaka Texts on Reasoning with the great scholar Patsap Lotsāwa Nyima Drak. At the important Kadampa center in Phenyül, he immersed himself in the Kadampa teachings, studying for six years with Geshé Sharawa and his student, Sherap Dorjé. Then he took full ordination from the preceptor Mal Dulzin Naljor Seng while Yeshé Lodrö acted as ritual master. Afterward Düsum Khyenpa trained extensively in the Vinaya and became an expert.

At the age of thirty, wishing to meet the Lord of Dharma Gampopa, he traveled to Daklha Monastery. For some two months he was not given an audience. When he finally met Gampopa, Düsum Khyenpa immediately offered ten silk scarves, and received some oral instruction along with a simple teaching on the stages of the path in the Kadampa tradition. Gampopa remarked, "I meditated on this and so should you." Following Gampopa's guidance and gathering all the positive conditions as a support, Düsum Khyenpa meditated just as his spiritual master had instructed.

Afterward, when Gampopa was bestowing a Hevajra empowerment, Düsum Khyenpa saw his teacher transformed into Hevajra, who appeared in a circle of light. The Karmapa received further oral instructions from texts teaching the path of method. When he meditated on them for nine days, warmth naturally blazed, and for nine months Düsum Khyenpa wore just a white cloth, while his hands were never free of perspiration. Immeasurable qualities of samādhi were born through this meditation. At Til Cave he meditated another four months, and at Phagdru for a month and five days, which brought him the mastery of calm abiding while numerous meditative experiences related to prāṇa (the inner winds) appeared. Again Düsum Khyenpa returned to be in the presence of his lama Gampopa, and for three years he meditated in great austerity. This practice made him famous among the eight hundred great meditators at Gampo as the one who was most capable of enduring hardships.

When Gampopa was staying at Jakok Monastery, Düsum Khyenpa offered his realizations to his teacher. The Lord of Dharma responded, "I had great hopes for you, but you're mistaken. You must meditate more." Düsum Khyenpa thought, "I'm not mistaken here, but this is my lama's command."

So he meditated another six months at Gampo. Nevertheless, no other indisputable realization or meditative experience arose that was new, more elevated, or at all different from his previous experience and realization. He again said to Gampopa, "Even though I've meditated for years, mind's nature would not essentially develop beyond this. So even though it's mistaken, my meditation is just this." Gampopa placed his hand on the crown of Düsum Khyenpa's head, saying, "Son, you have cut the ties to samsara." Introducing him into the abiding nature, that which truly is, Gampopa gave him the oral instruction of the wish-fulfilling gem, mind itself.

Düsum Khyenpa meet the great lord Rechungpa in Loro and stayed with him for forty days, after which Düsum Khyenpa recognized within himself, just like seeing his face in the mirror, the primordial wisdom that is coemergent bliss and emptiness.

Afterward, he returned to the Lord of Dharma Gampopa, who said, "Though my lama Milarepa possessed the whole range of positive qualities and vast modes of higher perceptions, he had not one atom of arrogance. In general, great meditators are not conceited about their good qualities." So saying, Gampopa gave Düsum Khyenpa his entire oral instructions, which he had not given to anyone else. The lama prophesied, "Son, go and practice at Kampo Gangra in Kham. Living beings throughout the three areas of Ü, Tsang, and Kham will be benefited."

At the age of fifty-five, Düsum Khyenpa traveled to Kampo Nenang in Kham. Though he had previously developed his practice of dream yoga, after he arrived there, his dreams were filled with nothing but radiant clarity, which he constantly experienced day and night without break. Düsum Khyenpa said, "Knowing this, the Lord of Dharma Gampopa made his prophecy. These experiences come from the blessing of accomplishing the lama's command." In this very place, Düsum Khyenpa founded the monastery of Kampo Nenang, the site related to his body. He spent nineteen years here and benefited inconceivable numbers of fortunate disciples.

Then, in 1185, when he was seventy-six, he went to Ledu Karma and founded Okmin Karma Gön (Akaniṣṭha Karma Monastery), the site related to Düsum Khyenpa's speech, which has benefited vast numbers of living beings. After staying there for a few years, he traveled to Central Tibet and went to meet Drigung Kyopa Jikten Sumgön at Bam Thang to take teachings from him. Düsum Khyenpa was inspired to say to him, "You are Nāgārjuna."

In 1189, when he was eighty, he founded Okmin Tsurphu (Akaniṣṭha Tsurphu), the site related to his heart-mind. In all these ways, he brought to perfection the two benefits for self and other.

For about three months before he passed away, portents continually appeared; in the sky there were rainbows, sounds, and lights, and earthquakes shook the ground, while many other unusual events occurred. Then Düsum Khyenpa said to his attendant Gang Lotsāwa, "Young one, you should stay here for a few years and keep my representations of body, speech, and mind from being dispersed. Do not let even one letter be scattered. I will also entrust all of these to the Dharma protectors." With these words, Düsum Khyenpa gave a prophecy that meant a reincarnation would indeed come.

After many auspicious signs arose, such as the sound of *damarus* filling the sky, in 1193 on the third day of the eleventh month of the Female Water Ox year, at the age of eighty-four, he withdrew the display of his emanation and departed in bliss for another pure realm.

Düsum Khyenpa's main disciples are known as the five sons with transmission, the four sons who hold the lineage, the four lights who served him, the four lamas, the four earlier sons, and the four later sons. There were also numerous great beings who had a Dharma connection with him.

1. The Second Karmapa Karma Pakṣi
2. Tashi Drak
3. Gyalwa Gyatso
4. Attendant Rinchen Pal
5. Mongolian Möngke Khan and His Khatun
6. Minister of the Khan
7. Damchan Kyebu Chenpo

The Second Karmapa Karma Pakṣi

1206–83

Thirteen years after Lord Düsum Khyenpa passed into nirvana, in the land of Drilung in Eastern Tibet, Karma Pakṣi was born as the youngest son of his father, Gyawang Tsurtsa, and his mother, Sengsa Mangkyi. This was in 1206, the year of the Fire Male Tiger in the third sixty-year cycle. The infant was given the name Chözin (Holder of the Dharma). From the age of five, he knew how to read very well. At the age of ten, he knew all the scriptures by just looking through them, so he did not need to rely on many teachers. When he reached the age of eleven, he first met Gyalsé Pomdrakpa Sönam Dorjé, who asked him, "Young monk, where do you come from?" "I'm coming from Western Tibet and going to Central Tibet," he replied.

"Aren't you my disciple?" Pomdrakpa asked. "Stay here. Don't go anywhere else."

That evening Pomdrakpa took him to the place where he would give an initiation, and there empowered Karma Pakṣi. Not moving away from mind itself, Karma Pakṣi became stable as a mountain. Lord Pomdrakpa introduced him to the nature of mind, so that Karma Pakṣi was able to realize a slight aspect of the essential nature of mind that had eluded him—it was like meeting someone he already knew.

Also at the age of eleven, Karma Pakṣi took the renunciate's vows from Gyalsé Pomdrakpa and received the name Palchenpo Chökyi Lama (Great and Glorious

Lama of the Dharma). Later, at his monastery, Pomdrakpa cared for this disciple as a father would his son, giving him immeasurable teachings of the genuine Dharma, including profound commentaries on the creation phase. The young monk thought, "I've been connected to this lama for many lifetimes. I should stay here and go nowhere else." So he remained practicing in accord with his lama's words, through which special experience and realization arose in his mind-stream.

Later, when Karma Pakṣi reached the right age, he took full ordination with Kathok Jampabum as the abbot, Rinpoché Pomdrakpa as the ritual master, and Chen Nga Mangphuwa as the one who privately asked him questions about his life.

On one occasion, Pomdrakpa said to Karma Pakṣi, "You are the one who bears the teachings of Lord Düsum Khyenpa. The activity of all the Kagyü rinpochés previous to me will come to you alone." Pomdrakpa empowered Karma Pakṣi as a master of the profound meaning contained in the ocean of teachings of the practice lineage. Pomdrakpa then passed away, displaying the way of those gone to bliss.

On another occasion at Silko Monastery, Karma Pakṣi said that the mandala of the face of Mahākāla had covered the earth and sky and continued to appear for a whole day. Mahākāla's eyes looked like suns and moons, and innumerable rays of light gathered in great masses while a thundering HŪṂ roared from his mouth. With this, limitless activity arose that could overpower all of apparent existence. Afterward, Karma Pakṣi went to the country of Korik, where he cured just by touching them many who were sick, crippled, or disabled in some way. His fame as a realized master spread in all directions.

Then Karma Pakṣi had a few corals that he sold for food; having made a powerful commitment, he practiced intensely for eleven years. His merit increased and the number of his disciples surged. When five hundred or more monks would gather, they would find food effortlessly, and Karma Pakṣi would bring them into the practice of meditation.

The Karmapa was able to send out as his agents Mahākāla and Mahākālī along with their retinue. Having subjugated the eight classes of gods and demons, he opened up a wide thoroughfare, directly manifesting his fierce activity as far as China and Jang. The noble Avalokiteśvara with eleven heads counselled him, "You should benefit beings through the activity of my six syllables, OṂ MAṆI PADME HŪṂ." The four types of ḍākiṇīs urged him on, "The time has come to train disciples with this Dharma of the six syllables," and so maturing his students through the practice of the six syllables became one of his main activities.

In order to restore the monastic seats of the Karmapa, Karma Pakṣi began by staying a year at Karma Gön. After repeated urging from Mahākāla and Mahākālī, who warned, "Tsurphu is about to be destroyed. It's time to go!" he departed for Tsurphu. When Karma Pakṣi went slightly astray on his way there, he urgently called upon the protector Mahākāla, who came to lead him with an army of his deities, arrayed in myriad divisions. Most of the people in the area witnessed this. When he arrived at Tsurphu, he found that the monastery had been destroyed by armies from the kingdoms of Ling and Beri; it was completely deserted. Karma Pakṣi stayed at Tsurphu a full six years, and due to him the teachings of Lord Düsum Khyenpa flourished.

When the prince Qubilai (ruled 1260–94) heard of the great qualities of the Lord of Dharma Karmapa, he sent a courier to invite the Karmapa to his court in China. At the age of fifty Karma Pakṣi agreed to go, having seen a sign that all his activity would be brought to perfection. In 1255 the prince Qubilai came in full battle array and met him in the low-lying country of Rongyul Serto. From there they proceeded to the tent palace, and all the subjects of the ruler paid Karma Pakṣi great respect. He blessed the prince, his consort, and their children. The prince supplicated Karma Pakṣi to stay with them always, but knowing that in the future the prince would fall under the sway of jealousy, Karma Pakṣi did not accept the invitation, which disappointed and displeased the prince.

Then Karma Pakṣi went to Minyak (Xia, the Tangut region), and during one hundred and one days, he finished the construction of a building known as the Magically Emanated Temple. Due to the words of Möngke Khan (Qubilai's older brother, ruled 1251–59), the rulers of China, Minyak, Mongolia, and Tibet heard of the Karmapa's fame, so he received many golden letters of invitation, which he accepted and traveled to numerous places. Previously, Möngke Khan followed the view and practice of Christianity, but through the influence of Karma Pakṣi, he turned away from this worship and became a Buddhist. For many days, Karma Pakṣi gave the khan empowerments and blessed him by introducing him to the four kāyas.

At this time, stupendous offerings were made from the treasury of Möngke Khan, and all prisoners were freed. The khan decreed that everyone under his command should refrain from killing on the days of the four great celebrations in the Buddhist year; they should keep the one-day fasting vows on the days of the new and full moon; those who follow the Mongolian religion of supplicating heaven (or an eternal god) and who make ritual offerings of fermented mare's milk should stay within the vows they hold; and finally, all should practice the ten virtues. For the khan, the realization of mahāmudrā dawned without effort. In all of China, Mongolia, Minyak, and Uighur, he ordered that old shrine halls and stupas be restored and new ones be built, and he provided much of what was necessary for these projects. The natural sound of the six syllables resounded in all directions, establishing people in maturation and liberation, and bringing many other benefits. Möngke Khan was the only Mongolian ruler to base the rules of his realm on the Dharma.

Subsequently, Karma Pakṣi skillfully related to Qubilai Khan. In 1260, his brother Möngke Khan passed away, and in the following year, Qubilai became the undisputed ruler. Mostly due to the influence of troublemakers around him, Qubilai Khan now dispatched a proclamation stating that the great master Karmapa should appear before him. When he gave this document to the executioners, some of them coughed up blood and died while their weapons shattered into pieces. This so angered the khan that he killed every one of the executioners.

After he had taken Karma Pakṣi prisoner, the khan tried to kill him as well.

> When they tried to burn him in a mass of flames,
> he lived right through it as a god of fire would.
> When they threw him into the river's flow,
> he sailed right along as a great fish would:
> the larger fish circled him and the little ones bowed down.
> When they gave him a cupful of poison to drink,
> he savored it just as a peacock would.
> When they flung him over the steepest cliff,
> he flew through the air as a royal bird would:
> the larger birds circled him and the little ones bowed down.

None of these attempts harmed Karma Pakṣi, so he was banished for more than two years to the shore of an ocean, devoid of drinking water and barren of trees. But rains of ambrosia fell and perfect fruits grew, transforming it into a land of the gods. Then, after being summoned back to the palace, he was shut into its shrine hall with an iron lock. For seven days he was left without any food, but many wisdom dākiṇīs held gaṇacakra feasts with magically emanated fruits and other nourishment that Karma Pakṣi enjoyed. He enabled others to see all of this as the walls turned transparent like crystal.

While Karma Pakṣi was undergoing these many trials, the Dharma protectors and guardians became enraged. The signs of their displeasure were many. A great number of the people who had created the rift between Qubilai Khan and Karma Pakṣi died in an instant. Many cities were burned to the ground, and other calamities occurred so that a good portion of the country was destroyed. Through the magical power of the wind, mountain peaks collapsed, cities were brought to ruin, and epidemics rained down everywhere. These severe reprisals actually occurred, instilling terror and awe in Qubilai Khan. With faith he bowed at the feet of Karma Pakṣi, and begging for forgiveness, confessed his mistakes. Karma Pakṣi brought the khan and his retinue into the Dharma, and the Karmapa's fame grew even greater than before.

From China Karma Pakṣi returned by stages to Tsurphu, where he would install Ogyenpa as his regent. When Ogyenpa arrived, he respectfully bowed to the Lord of Dharma Karmapa and sat on a fine seat that had been prepared. Karma Pakṣi turned to him, "Well, Ogyenpa, you had planned to go to Silmala and beyond, hadn't you? Are you aware that I summoned you with my bodhicitta?" Then Karma Pakṣi filled a metal basin with barley, stirred it with a cane whip blessed by Jinasāgara, and placed it on Ogyenpa's head, thus bestowing the empowerment. For three days, Karma Pakṣi gave Ogyenpa numerous oral instructions. Then the Karmapa said, "From the west, there will come one who wears the Black Hat." With this prophecy of his future reincarnation, Karma Pakṣi entrusted to Ogyenpa a special text and a Black Hat, saying: "Someone will come who can stand on his own two feet and fend for himself. Hand these over to him. From here, you should go to the south and benefit others extensively. We will meet soon." Finally, on the third day of the ninth month in the year of the Water Female Sheep (1283) of the fifth sixty-year cycle, even though he did not seem to be sick, his body appeared smaller and weaker than before. When those close to him asked about holding a long-life ceremony for him, Karma Pakṣi replied, "When the great Mount Sumeru crumbles, you can't prop it up with a stick. Remain silent and meditate."

Further, he said to Bön Rinpoché, "Until the reincarnation returns here, remain as the elder of the entire Sangha. For the sake of the monastery, work as its manager and care for the monks." Karma Pakṣi explained to a gathering of his disciples: "It is Ogyenpa who holds the transmission of the essential meaning. Möngke Khan is equal to me in abandonment and realization."

Karma Pakṣi's disciples also included the yogi Yeshé Wangchuk and Rinchen Pal; the realized masters who have special hats, Shaser, Shamar, and Shatrawa (yellow hat, red hat, and multicolored hat); the realized masters with *gowa* ("head") in their names, Takgowa, Sikgowa, and Domgowa; and also Nyenré Gendunbum, the bodhisattva Gyalwa, and Bön Rinpoché. Karma Pakṣi declared, "In this incarnation, I have benefited more my nonhuman disciples than my human ones." Karma Pakṣi said many amazing things like this.

1. The Third Karmapa Rangjung Dorjé
2. Bodhisattva Dripa Namsel
3. Nyanré Gendunbum
4. First Shamar Tokden Drakpa Sengé
5. Gyalwa Ritröpa Darma Gyaltsen

The Third Karmapa Rangjung Dorjé

1284–1339

Just eight days after Karma Pakṣi had passed into nirvana, he wished to enter his former body, but it had already been cremated. Then he thought, "I could transfer my consciousness to another body, and benefit living beings," so he entered the corpse of a thirteen-year-old boy, laid out between an elder couple. When his eyelids opened wide, the astonished couple watched the dead person's eyes coming to life. Thinking, "This is a very bad omen," they threw ashes into his eyes and pierced them with needles so he became totally blind. Realizing that he would not be able to help others, Karma Pakṣi left that body. Though he searched for another opportunity, he could find only a pigeon's corpse and realized that the time had not yet come to help others, so he remained in one-pointed meditation.

About four months later, on the eighth day of the first month in the year of the Wood Monkey from the fifth sixty-year cycle (1284), he was born in Tsaphu of Gungthang in Mangyul, located in Western Tibet. His father was the teacher Chöphel and his mother, Jomo Yangdren. At the age of three he said, "Make a hat like this out of black felt." Wearing the small hat, he sat on a stone throne in front of many other children and taught the text, *Introducing the Three Kāyas*, saying that he remembered it from before. The young boy also said, "I'm the Karmapa," and he often talked about what had happened previously and recounted other things that revealed he possessed the modes of higher perception. Both of his parents gave him the same devotion they would have offered him if he were actually the Karmapa, and they also spoke of him to others.

When Rangjung Dorjé was five years old, he wished to meet the realized master Ogyenpa Rinchen Pal, and so he departed with his parents and companions. In a vision, the Karmapa appeared to Ogyenpa and said, "You should know that I'm coming tomorrow." Ogyenpa got up very early and told the inner and outer circles of disciples, "Prepare a grand welcome!" Ogyenpa also thought, "We need to test this young boy." So he set up a seat higher than his own, figuring, "If this isn't my lama, he won't have the courage to sit here."

Then all who had gathered went to welcome their special guest. When the young boy arrived, he did not even prostrate to Ogyenpa but went straightaway to sit on the high seat. "Who are you?" Ogyenpa asked.

Raising his hand in the air, the boy replied, "My name is Karmapa. My fame has spread everywhere."

"Do you remember what you gave me?" Ogyenpa asked. "My Black Hat and a text!" was the quick reply.

"That's true." So Ogyenpa gave back to the young Karmapa his Black Hat and his text, *Introducing the Three Kāyas*, which he had remembered as a child. Donning the hat, the Karmapa gave a radiant smile and descended from the throne.

"Previously you were my lama. Now again I supplicate you to take care of me," and he prostrated to Ogyenpa. The young Karmapa was given the name Rangjung Dorjé (Naturally Arisen Vajra) along with empowerments, lay precepts, and abundant advice. With Kunden Sherap of the Trophu Kagyü acting as the abbot, the Karmapa took lay precepts. Afterward, he went to Tsurphu and met Nyenré.

In front of a bone-dry boulder, Rangjung Dorjé said, "If I am Karma Pakṣi, may a spring appear." As soon as he spoke, a copious spring gushed forth. Then he inserted a half-burned stick into the rock and said, "If I am Karma Pakṣi, this will grow. If not, nothing will happen." Instantly, the stick came to life. Even now, these two are famous as the water blessed by attainment and the tree blessed by attainment.

Mostly with the great master Nyenré, Rangjung Dorjé studied all the profound Dharma of the Kamtsang Kagyü, including the collections of the advice from Marpa, Milarepa, and Gampopa, and also all the teachings of the old and new schools of Tibet. Mainly with Jamyang Shakya Shönu, he studied texts belonging to the vehicle of characteristics and its commentarial tradition: The Seven Treatises on Validity and the *Compendium of Validity*, the *Compendium of Abhidharma*, and the *Treasury of Abhidharma* along with Asaṅga's treatises on the five levels, the five Dharmas of Maitreya, and the main Madhyamaka texts—the *Fundamental Wisdom of the Middle Way*, *Entering the Middle Way*, and the *Four Hundred Verses*—as well as many other works. In total, Rangjung Dorjé studied with one hundred and thirteen lamas and had the reputation of knowing every Dharma text that existed in Tibet.

When he turned eighteen, Rangjung Dorjé took full ordination. Acting as the abbot was Neten Shönu Jangchup (the fifth in a line of abbots from Gendun Gangpa), and the ritual master was the learned Gendun Rinchen. With both of them Rangjung Dorjé studied the words of the Buddha and the treatises related to the Vinaya.

Rangjung Dorjé then traveled to Karma Gön. Once, when he was staying in the monastery's place of practice known as Yang Gön, he had a vision of Vimalamitra, who dissolved into the space between the Karmapa's eyebrows. From that time onward he knew clearly the words and the meaning of the Great Perfection (*Dzokchen*). The Karmapa then traveled on to Kampo Nenang and other places, caring for people by settling important disputes, eliminating the fear of fire, and reversing mantric spells. When he went to monasteries belonging to other traditions, such as the Sakya, he engaged many of their masters in conversation about the Dharma. He met Kunkhyen Dölpopa, who at that time was partial to the view of intrinsic emptiness (*rangtong*). Rangjung Dorjé prophesied, however, that later Dölpopa would realize a very special view, which turned out to be that of extrinsic emptiness (*shentong*).

Rangjung Dorjé's compositions include the treatise the *Profound Inner Meaning* and its auto-commentary; the two shorter texts *Distinguishing Consciousness and Wisdom* and *A Treatise on Buddha Nature*; the *Compendium of Astrology*, and so forth. His collected works encompass sixteen volumes.

When Rangjung Dorjé was forty-eight, the Yuan dynasty ruler Tuq-Temür Khan (ruled 1328–32) invited him to the court, requesting the Lord of Dharma to leave Kongpo. Even though the Karmapa went quickly, Toq-Temür Khan passed away on the twelfth day of the eighth Tibetan month in 1332. Knowing this would happen, Rangjung Dorjé performed ceremonies to purify the khan's negativity and transfer his consciousness to a higher level. About two months later, the Karmapa arrived at the royal palace. The nephew of Toq-Temür Khan, Ratna Śrī, along with his retinue paid their great respects to Rangjung Dorjé. Prophesying that this khan would also have a short life, Rangjung Dorjé nurtured him with empowerments and teachings on the transference of consciousness. One month later, Ratna Śrī passed away, and Rangjung Dorjé again performed the ceremony of purifying negativity.

Rangjung Dorjé placed the older brother Toghan Temür (reigned 1333–70) on the throne at the royal seat. When the khan was traveling from Metsé to the great palace, millions of people gathered to welcome him—so many thronged the city that no one could clear a path through the crowds. When the Karmapa came wearing the Black Hat and reciting Avalokiteśvara's mantra, a path naturally opened for him wherever he went throughout the city. To greet the Karmapa, the great khan stood before an immense tent and bowed with deep respect at the Karmapa's feet. The one giving offerings (the khan) and the one receiving them (the Karmapa) then went together to the palace where the ruler and all his ministers were brought into the Dharma. Afterward, Rangjung Dorjé returned to Tibet.

For two years, the khan repeatedly sent letters of invitation and copious gifts to Rangjung Dorjé, so he returned to China for a second visit, journeying to the great palace at the age of fifty-four. Once, when only a minister, the khan, and the Karmapa were present, the Karmapa bestowed on the khan a long-life empowerment and long-life water, which enabled him to become the longest-lived ruler to occupy the royal seat.

Around this time, due to the misbehavior of some monks from China and Amdo, a few of the local leaders became hostile to the Dharma. They destroyed many monasteries, forced the monks to disrobe, and announced an impending war. Through his fearless courage, Rangjung Dorjé intimidated them all. Terrified of him, they rebuilt the temples they had ruined and made other reparations. Due to Rangjung Dorjé's efforts, the victorious teachings shone with brilliance like the sun.

When the Karmapa had passed through fifty-six winters, on the fourteenth day of the sixth month in the year of the Earth Hare (1339), he showed the way of dissolving the mandala of his form into the expanse of all phenomena. The next night, when the full moon shone forth, the face of the precious Lord of Dharma appeared within it. The gatekeepers noticed this and conveyed the wonder to the khan. The news spread so almost everyone—the khan, his ministers, and many others—witnessed the presence of the Karmapa in the full moon. The khan said, "Create a silver painting just like this." The image became known as "Rangjung's Visage in the Moon" or "The Image of His Face in the Moon." Its blessing was identical to that of his actual presence. In Tibet, the realized master Drakpa Sengé saw in his pure vision the Lord of Dharma wearing golden robes and walking back and forth on the moon. When Drakpa Sengé questioned him, Rangjung Dorjé replied, "I'm going to Tuṣita," and departed into space. Through pure vision, the Karmapa revealed many wonders like these.

Among his students were the First Shamar, the realized master Drakpa Sengé, the learned and realized Yung Tönpa (Ogyenpa's reincarnation), and the realized master Gönpo Gyaltsen. The names are given more extensively in Rangjung Dorjé's biographies.

1. The Fourth Karmapa Rölpai Dorjé
2. Attendant Rinchen Pal
3. Sangwadüpa
4. Tokden Gönpo Gyaltsen
5. Five Indian Yogis

The Fourth Karmapa Rölpai Dorjé

1340–83

Rölpai Dorjé was born to his father, Sönam Döndrup, and his mother, Tsöndru Gyen, on the eighth day of the third month in the year of the Iron Dragon belonging to the sixth of the sixty-year cycles (1340). Right away, the infant sat up straight and recited Avalokiteśvara's mantra and the Sanskrit alphabet. When his umbilical cord was cut, the entire region was filled with the scent of perfume.

At the age of three, the young boy said to his mother, "I am Karma Pakṣi. I have come because there are many disciples to be trained in this world. Look! I will do the yogic exercises that take us beyond death," and he demonstrated them.

"When I did these in your womb, they made you bounce up and down and breathe hard."

"If you are Karma Pakṣi," she asked, "then are you not Rangjung Dorjé?" "They are the same," he replied.

When he was six, the young incarnation went to Drachi Temple and said to Drogön, "You have my crown and footprint. Bring them here!" And Drogön offered them to him. The following day, the young boy wore the Black Hat and said, "I am Düsum Khyenpa. I am also Karma Pakṣi. I am the one who tamed China and Mongolia. There are still disciples who need training. One of my emanations is with Lodrö Rinchen, another is in the eastern pure realm of Abhirati, and here in this world I myself have come."

Beginning in his ninth year, Rölpai Dorjé studied with many lamas, such as the realized master Gön Gyalwa, and trained in many practices, such as the six yogas of Naropa, Jinasāgara, Cakrasaṃvara, and Vajravārāhī.

Rölpai Dorjé received empowerments, reading transmissions, and key instructions from the old and new traditions. At the age of thirteen, he traveled to Central Tibet. The ruler of the provinces of Ü and Tsang paid him great honor and offered his deep respect. Passing through Daklha Monastery and others, he arrived at Tsurphu, where he went to meet Yung Tönpa. Rölpai Dorjé told him about the previous Karmapa, completely convincing Yung Tönpa that he was his reincarnation. The Karmapa received all the empowerments and key instructions of the precious tantras from Yung Tönpa's line of transmission.

When he was fourteen, Rölpai Dorjé received the lay precepts as well as the novice vows from the master Sönam Bum and was given the name Pal Chökyi Drakpa (Glorious Fame of the Dharma). He studied numerous cycles of teachings on the genuine Dharma of the Vinaya.

As the young boy's fame spread, Tsalpa Situ and many others were saying that he was definitely the previous Lord of Dharma. The emperor placed his palms together and shed tears. The same happened to all the high ministers who came into the Karmapa's presence. When the Mongolian ruler heard his name, he also shed tears. Everyone was deeply touched.

In 1357, when he was eighteen, Rölpai Dorjé took full ordination with his previous abbot and ritual master, and this time the learned Shönu Pal was the private questioner. Down to the slightest detail, the Karmapa followed the Mahāyāna vows of individual liberation and the rules of the Vinaya common to the foundational and great vehicles. The mere scent of meat or alcohol was not allowed near him nor could they come within his sight. His retinue was not permitted to perform feasts with meat and alcohol, and so forth.

Rölpai Dorjé mastered dream yoga. If he wanted to look at certain texts, for example, they would be opened and arranged nearby him. When he awoke from dream yoga, he had memorized them all, so he did not need to study much. Karma Trinlepa said that among the first seven generations of Karmapas who wore the Black Hat, Rölpai Dorjé was the most learned in the Madhyamaka view, in logic, and in poetry.

Once, five yogis came from India. "We're going to the Five-Peaked Mountain (Wutai Shan) in China," they said. "This stupa with its Buddha image was carved from the Bodhi Tree by noble Nāgārjuna. We're entrusting it to your safekeeping for a while. Until the five of us had come together, we were asked not to give this to anyone." They offered him what came to be known as the Jowo Gandhola. These five yogis were considered emanations of Dharma protectors, because later, when people searched everywhere, not one of them could be found. From that time onward, the Jowo Gandhola became the most important object of offerings at Tsurphu.

At one time Toghan Temür along with his sons sent an imperial courier to invite Rölpai Dorjé to the court. Turning his face toward China, he departed Tsurphu at the age of nineteen. After he arrived, the Karmapa satisfied with empowerments and Dharma teachings all the faithful, led by the khan and his offspring. In particular, the prince became learned in studying the explanations and commentaries on the tantras and major texts from India.

In 1362 Rölpai Dorjé returned to Tibet. In Kamchu and other places, people feared the outbreak of an epidemic. The master Guigungpa asked Rölpai Dorjé, "Is there some way to avert it?"

He replied, "I have the skillful means to do it. Do not wake me up." Rölpai Dorjé appeared to go to sleep. While the master stayed by the Karmapa, a huge noise—*tsak*! *tsak*!—came from the rooftop.

The Karmapa woke up and asked, "Did something like an omen happen up on the roof?"

"Yes, it did."

"I emanated a huge garuḍa whose wings covered the entire land. He ate and scattered the many nonhuman spirits who have power over the disease. Once this garuḍa had burned them up in the pit of his stomach, he landed here on the roof. The epidemic has been brought to an end." And so it was.

When Rölpai Dorjé was traveling in the country of Tsongkha to the east, he gave novice vows and also the name Kunga Nyingpo to Jé Losang Drakpa (Jé Tsongkhapa). The Karmapa conveyed to him the prophetic advice that Jé Losang Drakpa should go to the central provinces of Ü and Tsang.

While Rölpai Dorjé was teaching, he said to close disciples on separate occasions, "In China, the body of the previous Lord of Dharma was purified by the fires of sandalwood and aloe wood. We don't have these in Tibet, but we can use our juniper instead. In the north, firewood is probably hard to find, so cut a lot of juniper and bring it with us." This they did. The party traveled to the north, arriving at the foot of a mountain in a very isolated northern area. The Karmapa prophesied, "If a very pure, fully ordained monk were cremated on the peak of this mountain, the Chinese army would not come to Tibet for a long time."

Finally, at the age of forty-four, on the night of the fifteenth day of the seventh month in the year of the Water Female Pig from the sixth cycle of sixty years, Rölpai Dorjé circumambulated his numerous representations of body, speech, and mind fifty-two times. As the last early light of dawn appeared amid many wondrous signs, Rölpai Dorjé demonstrated the way of dissolving physical form into the expanse of all phenomena. As his corpse was being cremated on this mountain peak called Shak, a rainbow tent floated above it, and many other amazing sights occurred. A stupa was built here, known as the One Hundred Thousand Bodies of the Karmapa in Shak.

Rölpai Dorjé's main disciples were Shamar Khachö Wangpo, master Guigung Rinchen Pal, Karma Könshön, Situ Drungchen, Yölwa Yeshé Pal, and Kashi Dzinpa Rinchen Pal. His students are too numerous to name them all.

1. The Fifth Karmapa Deshin Shekpa
2. Attendant
3. Jampalyang
4. Shrine Master and an Assistant
5. Ming Emperor Yongle and his Ministers

The Fifth Karmapa Deshin Shekpa

1384–1415

In the year of the Wood Mouse from the sixth sixty-year cycle, the Karmapa was born in the Nyingma area of the Nyenpa region. His father was the tantric practitioner Guru Rinchen and his mother was Lhamo Kyé. While he was still in her womb, the six-syllable mantra of Avalokiteśvara, the Sanskrit alphabet, and OṂ ĀḤ HŪṂ could be heard coming from his mother's abdomen. Many such amazing signs occurred. Even ordinary people said, "For sure the Lord of Dharma Karmapa has come here," and their words spread. About half a month after his birth, Lopön Guigung sent Khenchen Gönlön to offer tea and the traditional offerings for a new incarnation: robes, a blending of barley flour and butter, daily necessities, and other items. The infant caught hold of Khenchen's index finger, climbed onto his lap, and delighted him, so he was convinced this was the right child. When the boy was five months old, the great Lopön Guigung himself came to meet him.

While Shamar Khachö Wangpo was on the way to see the Karmapa, Geshé Shakdor told the child several times, "Today a realized Lord of Dharma is approaching."

"He's not coming today," the boy responded, "I'll only meet him tomorrow afternoon." And that is what happened. Khachö Wangpo brought the boy many gifts and also the Black Hat of his previous incarnation. The boy picked it up and put it on his head. It was a perfect fit, neither too large nor too small, which people found amazing.

Another time, when the Karmapa was playfully inserting a riding whip again and again into a massive rock, he made an indentation with the shape of a tent peg. "Break this open," he commanded. When they did, there appeared a creature shaped like a lung and about eighteen inches long. It was covered on the outside with black bugs and filled to the brim on the inside with white bugs. The Karmapa spat on them, and through the force of his piercing samādhi, they all died. Rainbows and showers of blossoms appeared.

"Burn that corpse," he said.

"What's the story of this?" he was asked.

"Previously, in the time of Rölpai Dorjé, a lama from here stole offerings that had been made for the living and the dead. He asked me to lead him out of the hell realms, and I agreed. The black bugs are the deceased whose offerings the lama had consumed; the white bugs are the living whose offerings he had consumed. As retribution, they have eaten his body. All of this happened just as I had foretold, and I led them into the pure realm of Sukhāvatī." Pawo Tsuklak Trengwa (1504–66) wrote in his *Origins of Dharma* that during his time, one could still see actual traces of the bugs.

At first, the Karmapa studied mahāmudrā, the six yogas of Naropa, and the six applications with the great Lopön Guigung, and he also received teachings on a great number of commentaries, reading transmissions, empowerments, and key instructions. Subsequently, the Karmapa relied on Khachö Wangpo as his main lama and studied all the profound Dharma of the tantras, such as Mahākāla, Jinasāgara, and Vajrayoginī. Taking them directly into his experience, he brought to perfection both abandonment and realization.

When he was seven, the Karmapa took novice vows from the important scholar Nyakphuwa Sönam Sangpo (an emanation of the arhat Bakula), the master Gyaltsen Pal, and others, and received the name Dharmaśrībhadra or Chöpal Sangpo (Excellent One of the Glorious Dharma). He also studied the Vinaya with these teachers. Kashipa Rinchen Pal was invited from Sangphu to the Karmapa's encampment, where he taught the Tripiṭaka to the Karmapa, who studied it extensively.

When he was nineteen, the Karmapa took full ordination from the scholar Nyakphuwa and the master Yönten Lodrö. Also present were eighty monks who had studied the collection of scriptures (the Vinaya, the Sutras, and the Abhidharma along with their related texts). It became widely known that in Tibet the fully ordained monks performing ceremonies were excellent and numerous.

According to Chinese history, at the age of thirty-five the Mongolian emperor Toghan Temür took over China. Five years after the Fourth Karmapa Rölpai Dorjé returned to Tibet, there was a revolt in China, and this khan returned to Mongolia.

For a short while, the Chinese ruler Taizu was in power, and then the great Ming emperor Yongle gained sovereignty over all of China, Mongolia, and Minyak. While the empire was at peace, the emperor heard of the Lord of Dharma's fame and, extremely impressed, invited the Karmapa to court repeatedly. Finally, at the age of twenty-two, Deshin Shekpa left Central Tibet while the emperor was still sending requests for him to come quickly.

When Deshin Shekpa finally arrived at the palace in 1407, three hundred fully caparisoned elephants carrying members of the Sangha came out to greet him. On that day, the supreme emperor came from the palace to its outer wall. He offered the Karmapa a thousand-spoked wheel made of gold and a white conch shell that turned clockwise. When the Lord of Dharma took out a similar white conch shell from the folds of his robes and gave it to the emperor, his faith increased even more.

The next day, the Karmapa was invited into the great palace. Greeting him were three elephants adorned with as much gold as they could carry, and three hundred elephants loaded with a rich display of decorations. On five elephants, fully ordained monks in yellow robes held offerings aloft. Nine important princes, three thousand senior court officials, one hundred thousand members of the nobility, and twelve military divisions with their armor and a variety of weapons all came out to welcome the Karmapa. The emperor himself came out to the main gate to receive him. Spiritual biographies of the Karmapas tell of this event at length.

From the fifth day of the following month until the eighteenth day, twelve mandalas were created, including Jinasāgara, Guhyasamāja, and Hevajra, and their sādhanas were practiced. The emperor and empress came for one whole day, and the Karmapa gave them empowerments. During these days, a rainbow tent appeared; the emperor, who was the sponsor, had a vision of the sixteen arhats; nectar fell from the top of a tree; and a golden flower bloomed on the crown of a juniper. From the time the ceremonies started until they finished, rainbows appeared in various shapes, and blossoms fell in plentiful showers. Everyone present witnessed these events.

Many wonders appeared, starting from the moment the emperor met the Karmapa through to the time when the Lord of Dharma was giving the emperor teachings and performing ceremonies. At the command of the emperor, skilled artists painted images that perfectly reflected the days of miracles on a long, silk scroll painting. The events were described in five languages—Chinese, Mongolian, Tibetan, Uighur, and Turkish—and the scroll was offered to Deshin Shekpa. These special records of the pure visions became famous as the One Hundred and Eight Wonders. Later, after the emperor received an explanation of mahāmudrā and the six yogas, he practiced them and attained a very special experience and realization.

Years before this, during the ceremony of taking vows, the Karmapa had received the name Dharmaśrībhadra from his abbot; however, the emperor offered the Karmapa another name: Deshin Shekpa Rinpoché Chökyi Gyalpo Nupchoki Jampa Chenpo Shiwa Wangchuk (Precious Tathāgata, King of the Dharma, Great Maitreya of the West, Peaceful and Powerful Buddha). Further the emperor offered the Karmapa a proclamation made of one hundred beaten gold coins and also a crystal seal known as the Wish-Fulfilling Gem. In this way, the Fifth Karmapa became famous as Deshin Shekpa (Tathāgata). To three lamas who were with the Karmapa—Drongbu Gö Shiwa, the master Kashipa Rinchen Pal, and the great abbot Gönlön—the emperor gave the important rank of the Great Goshri along with a gold seal and a hat with oval crystals in front. About one thousand Chinese monks who had committed serious offenses had been put in prison where they lived under a death sentence. The emperor pardoned and freed them all.

At one time, the emperor suggested to the Karmapa, "You should merge all Dharma traditions into your own and every year make an extensive Dharma tour of Central, Western, and Eastern Tibet."

The Lord of Dharma replied, "One Dharma tradition alone cannot work with all the various tendencies of living beings. Due to the Buddha's compassion, individuals enter the Dharma according to their specific inclinations." And so the Karmapa did not take up the emperor's advice.

Later, due to circumstances that had created a division between Tibet and China, a Chinese army was on the verge of invading Tibet. Deshin Shekpa repeatedly gave the emperor his counsel, and finally the emperor placed the words of his lama on the crown of his head and postponed the war, preventing future suffering for the Chinese and present suffering for the Tibetans. The Karmapa's kindness was immense.

After having benefited a great number of people and other forms of life in China, Mongolia, Uighur, and Minyak, Deshin Shekpa turned toward Tibet. When one of the members of the Great Encampment engaged in malicious behavior, Masé Tokden said, "This person should be severely reprimanded one time." The Karmapa responded, "I have never experienced hatred within, so I don't know how to get angry. You just follow through with your thought and act quickly." Having said this, Deshin Shekpa thought about giving up his body.

When he was thirty-two, in the year of the Wood Female Sheep (1415), during the waxing moon of the eighth month, the Karmapa displayed the manner of becoming extremely ill. Though he was offered a long-life ceremony, he said, "My thoughts have already turned to the vicinity of Karma Gön in Eastern Tibet. Pray to me. I will hold you with compassion." On the fifteenth of that month during the day, his mind was gathered into the expanse of all phenomena. When Deshin Shekpa's precious body was cremated, it left images in the forms of Cakrasaṃvara and Hevajra as well as a very large number of relics. Many other wondrous signs occurred as well.

Since the Karmapa lived only to the age of thirty-two, we have just a few texts from him. His main students included Goshri Rinchen Pal; Goshri Döndrup Öser (also known as Jamyang Chenpo); Goshri Chökyi Gyaltsen (the first in the line of Situ Rinpochés); Kashipa Rinchen Pal; the Third Shamar, Chöpal Yeshé; and Masé Tokden. This Karmapa was unusual in that he had many students who were realized masters able to help others.

1. The Sixth Karmapa Thongwa Dönden
2. Attendant
3. Yangchenma
4. The Third Shamar Chöpal Yeshé
5. Rongtön Sheja Kunsik

The Sixth Karmapa Thongwa Dönden

1416–53

In accord with the previous Karmapa's statement that he had turned his thoughts to the area around Karma Gön, he was born nearby at a place called Ngomtö on the eighth day of the second month in the year of the Fire Monkey (1416). His father was the tantric practitioner Gojo Samdrup, and his mother was Dongja Pematso. As soon as he was born, he sat up straight, and looking at his mother, he laughed. A beautiful fragrance filled the land.

A disciple of the previous Karmapa, Ngompa Jadrelpa, heard about the signs indicating that a reincarnation had been born, so he disguised himself as a beggar and went to find him. A month and four days after the boy's birth while he was traveling, Ngompa Jadrelpa met the infant with his parents, who were begging. As soon as the child saw him, he made many happy gestures and recited the Sanskrit alphabet. The beggar secretly asked the young one, "Who are you?" Holding onto Jadrelpa's index finger, he replied, "I am unborn, beyond all expression," and he spoke five lines of verse. Convinced that this child was the reincarnation, Jadrelpa offered to serve him. He invited the child to his quarters nearby, where they looked over statues, texts, and stupas together. When the child saw one image with the Black Crown, he smiled. "Who is that?" he was asked. Pointing his index finger at his heart, he said, "It's me! It's me!" Some time later, on the way to Karma

Gön, the young incarnation scattered blessed grains and stopped a smallpox epidemic. Gazing at a butter lamp, he saw Avalokiteśvara and Jinasāgara at the tip of its wick. When he was consecrating a scroll painting, seven of the grains remained suspended in the air.

The monks at Karma Gön recited many Mantrayāna pujas. The Karmapa asked them, "What's the reason for doing these?"

They did not know and replied, "We don't have manuals for them."

"I'm ready to compose them," the Karmapa promised.

As if bestowed by his supreme yidam deity, he wrote many manuals, which covered, for example, the Vajra Expanse, Cakrasaṃvara, Vajrayoginī, and Mahākāla's lama dance with drum and melody.

The Sixth Karmapa's kindest root lama was Sokön Rigpai Raldri. When Thongwa Dönden was a youth, Sokön was invited to the Great Encampment. With him the Karmapa first studied the Prajñāpāramitā sutras and became quite an expert. Afterward, he studied an ocean of texts from the sutras and tantras, the Kangyur and Tengyur, and the tradition of major treatises, attaining perfect knowledge of them. He received a vast number of empowerments and practiced a vast number of sādhanas. When he was receiving an empowerment for Vajrayoginī, he had a vision of her and her retinue of four. He had an immense number of such spacious, pure visions.

At the age of eight, he took lay precepts and novice vows from Khenchen Sönam Sangpo, who came from Gendun Gangpa. Khenchen Gönlön asked this special lama, Khenchen Sönam Sangpo: "I request that you will again be the abbot when the Karmapa takes full ordination. I also pray that until then, your life will be stable and firm." Khenchen Sönam Sangpo agreed to both requests. When the Karmapa was nearing the right age for taking the vows, a quarrel broke out between an imperial messenger and those close to the Karmapa. This messenger lied to Khenchen Sönam Sangpo, saying, "Those close to the Karmapa have already finished giving him the vows of full ordination." Sönam Sangpo responded, "Is that so?" His face turned dark, and three days later he passed away.

Although the Karmapa's actual name was Chödrak Sangpo, he became known as Thongwa Dönden (Beneficial to See). Since just seeing his face brought infinite well-being and happiness to others, those who turned to him supplicated, "I pray to the tulku Thongwa Dönden," and that became his name.

One time, in front of the Jowo in Lhasa, the master Kunkhyen Rongtön and others were giving vast and profound teachings to tens of thousands of ordained and lay people. Having great faith in Kunkhyen Rongtön, the Karmapa gave him praise based on his own pure vision. It began, "Above you, the gods hold aloft a fine white umbrella." The Karmapa took teachings on the sutra tradition and also key instructions from Kunkhyen Rongtön, who said, "I have the Buddha as my student," spreading his praise like a lion roaring.

When Thongwa Dönden was thirty-seven, he stayed at Tsé Lhagang. Those familiar with the hidden omens said that for a time he would have a severe obstacle, so Lopön Sangyé Sengé offered a long-life ceremony. The Karmapa said, "These days I won't have any problems. I'll take responsibility for living another nine months."

Then he told Goshri Rinpoché Paljor Döndrup (the first Gyaltsap Rinpoché), "Do not let the seals on these representations of body, speech, and mind deteriorate in any way." When Thongwa Dönden was thirty-eight in the year of the Water Bird, on the morning of the eighth day in the first month, he said, "Now I, too, will enter the ranks of the previous Kagyü lamas." For the benefit of his students, he recited the supplication:

> Precious One who embodies all the buddhas,
> Thongwa Dönden, you are compassion itself;
> I supplicate you. Please look upon me with compassion.
> May this prayer bring an unending shower of your blessings.

Then his mind demonstrated the way of entering into nirvana. Of his many students, the main ones were Goshri Rinpoché Paljor Döndrup and Kunkhyen Jampal Sangpo.

1. The Seventh Karmapa Chödrak Gyatso
2. Dorjé Namjom
3. The Fourth Shamar Chen Nga Chödrak
4. Panchen Shakya Chokden
5. The Second Situ Tashi Namgyal

The Seventh Karmapa Chödrak Gyatso

1454–1506

As the previous Karmapa was about to pass away, he gave Goshri Rinpoché a prophecy in the form of a Last Testament. In accord with this, and also with the predictions of Tsurphu Jamyang Chenpo and Kunkhyen Bengar Jampal, the Seventh Karmapa was born in Ngechida to his father, Drakpa Paldrup, and his mother, Lhamo Kyi. This was on the morning of the fifteenth day of the first month in the year of the Wood Dog from the eighth sixty-year cycle. Many wondrous signs occurred, such as rainbow lights and rains of flowers. As soon as he was born, he said, "A la la" and smiled. Six naturally arisen signs appeared on his body: images of flowers could be seen on his skin; in the center of the ridge at the back of his head appeared an image of Vajradhara; his nerves traced the letter A at his heart; a source of dharmas and a wheel arose at his secret place; and there were wheels on both his feet.

Fifteen days after the Karmapa was reborn, the elderly lama Chö Paljor came from Ngö and placed before the infant the previous Karmapa's robes and crown along with the robes and crown of a past realized master. The infant stretched out his hand and straightaway reached for those belonging to the previous Karmapa. When the child was nine months old, he met Goshri Rinpoché, who gave him the name Rangjung Kunkhyen Chökyi Gyalpo (Naturally Arisen, Omniscient King of

Dharma). Subsequently he was installed on the lion throne of Tsurphu, Ornament of the World.

When the young incarnation was five, Goshri Rinpoché offered him an Amitāyus empowerment and taught him the Tibetan and Chinese alphabets. When he was nine, the Karmapa was offered the five lay precepts and the bodhisattva vow by Goshri Rinpoché. During these ceremonies, the sky was filled with rainbow-colored lights and copious rains of flowers.

At the age of twelve, in the presence of the Jowo Gandhola as well as a statue of the Buddha known as Thupa Chulön, and other precious representations of the Dharma, he took novice vows with Kunkhyen Bengar Sangpo as the abbot and Goshri Chenpo as the ritual master. He received the name Chödrak Gyatso Palsangpo (Ocean of Dharma Fame, Glorious and Excellent). He studied the sutras and treatises of the Vinaya with the abbot. Afterward, the Karmapa did not disdain even the most subtle points of discipline, which is the foundation for training, and put them all into practice.

From the time he was seven days old and starting to teach, whatever the Karmapa taught flowed freely from him—nothing held him back—so in this life, he did not need to rely on many lamas. From another point of view, however, considering the continuum of reading transmissions, he turned with respect to both Bengar Jampal Sangpo and Goshri Paljor Döndrup. The Karmapa's previous incarnation, Thongwa Dönden, had contemplated his next incarnation and the need he would have for reading transmissions, so this Sixth Karmapa sent the bodhisattva Paljor Döndrup around to listen to almost all the Dharma that existed in Tibet. It was due to this kindness and forethought that the Seventh Karmapa could receive so many transmissions, beginning with the Kangyur and Tengyur. Until he reached the age of thirty-one, the Karmapa received discourses on the Dharma from Paljor Döndrup;

they were together like a body and its shadow. Such a teacher and student, both of whom had both studied the Dharma so extensively, were extremely rare in Tibet.

Chödrak Gyatso traveled widely to many places, including Kongpo, Lithang, Nenang, Khawakar, Dartsedo, Amdo, and Bomnyak, and he further circulated through the area known as the Six Ridges of Eastern Tibet. He founded many monasteries and places of practice and also brought into harmony those who were quarreling so that significant disturbances did not occur for twenty-five years. Bandits stopped their robbing for three years. Groups of villages and benefactors in great numbers made the commitment to recite one, ten, or one hundred million mani mantras.

In his pure vision, the Karmapa sometimes met Hayagrīva, at other times Jinasāgara or Cakrasaṃvara. He also saw Vajrayoginī, the Four-Armed Avalokiteśvara, the Eleven-Headed Avalokiteśvara, and Mañjuśrī.

Chödrak Gyatso assembled *The Twenty-Branch Mönlam* (a book of prayers), which was recited on the days of the four great celebrations in the Buddhist calendar. In particular, it was chanted during the first fifteen days of the month of miracles, which is the first month according to the Tibetan calendar. During the mornings of the Mönlam, the Karmapa would stand next to his low seat and bow in front of a wondrous and enormous number of precious Dharma objects unequalled in the entire world. He would then sit down to recite the great prayers. During this time all the lay people of the Great Encampment could see the Karmapa, and also hear him recite the dedications for the living and the dead. In the afternoon, great dramas were staged based on narratives from the Buddha's previous lives; they also depicted the histories of accomplished practitioners from Tibet and China, and showed how they came into this world. The dramas also portrayed the stories of the cakravartin kings and others as well.

Chödrak Gyatso always sat in vajra posture with his hands in the meditation mudra and his gaze unwavering—the Karmapa never left his samādhi. He did not engage in mundane conversation; aside from some discourse about the Dharma, he generally did not talk much. Since it was so difficult and rare to meet him, during the celebration of the Buddha's miracles when he could be seen, the faithful came just to catch a glimpse of him. The members of the Great Encampment came in the morning, and in the afternoon people came in droves from the surrounding villages.

At the Great Encampment, the disciplinary rules were strict and rigorously enforced, and so studying, reflecting, and meditating were very powerful and at a high level. If parties took place nearby the encampment, meat was not allowed, and it could not be carried inside either. The best practitioners gave up alcohol completely, and the least gave it up for one day. Due to this discipline, though many lived in the Great Encampment, problems such as fights and bullying did not occur, and everyone maintained their faith.

From Chödrak Gyatso's spiritual biography we know that he composed over eight volumes of texts, including the extensive treatise on logic called *An Ocean of Literature on Logic*; a commentary on the *Ornament of Realization* (*Abhisamaya-alaṃkāra*) called *A Lamp for the Three Worlds*; and *Rituals for the Three Foundations of the Vinaya*.

In these many ways, Chödrak Gyatso benefited the teachings and living beings. When he was fifty-three, at the time of the New Year in the year of the Fire Tiger from the eighth sixty-year cycle (1506), people earnestly requested to see him. On the twelfth of the first month, the inner circle met with him, and during the day of the fourteenth, the public saw him as he sat on his throne. A full hundred thousand monks and lay people were present as the Karmapa said, "My nirmāṇakāya has already withdrawn. This is the sambhogakāya." So saying, he put on the six sambhogakāya ornaments made of pearls and revealed to everyone the appearance of a cakravartin king. Previously, he had given to Situ Rinpoché a letter that was his Last Testament, clearly indicating where his reincarnation would appear and who his parents would be. Nevertheless, this evening he placed on his table a letter of his Last Testament that was not so clear. At daybreak, his mind departed for the expanse of all phenomena.

His disciples included Gyaltsap Tashi Namgyal, Shamar Chenga Chödrak, Situ Tashi Paljor, Drikung Wang Rinpoché, Sangyé Nyenpa, Dulmo Tashi Öser, Panchen Shakya Chokden, Karma Trinlepa Chenpo, and also Gö Lotsāwa Shönu Pal, Shalu Lotsāwa Chökyong Sangpo, and Tsang Nyön, Ü Nyön and Druk Nyön Kunlek. Vast numbers of disciples made a Dharma connection with Chödrak Gyatso.

1. The Eighth Karmapa Mikyö Dorjé
2. Tsepakmé Tsasum Drildrup
3. Khenpo Chödrup Sengé
4. The Third Gyaltsap Drakpa Paljor
5. The Second Pawo Tsuklak Trengwa
6. Attendant

The Eighth Karmapa Mikyö Dorjé

1507–54

The previous Karmapa wrote a prediction signaling that his next incarnation would be born in the vicinity of Karma Gön to his father, Jampa, and his mother, Lama. The prediction letter was given to the Third Situ Tashi Paljor and the Second Goshri Gyaltsap Tashi Namgyal. Just as the letter indicated, the Karmapa was born near the seat of glorious Karma Gön in Satam Drong in the countryside of Karati Cave on the right side of the river Ngom as it flows downstream. He was born to his father, A Jam, and his mother, Lama Drön, on the fourth day of the eleventh month in the year of the Fire Hare from the ninth sixty-year cycle (1507). As soon as he was born, the infant said, his eyes wide awake, "I'm the Karmapa."

When Situ Rinpoché arrived in the region, the father A Jam went to meet him. "I have an extraordinary child," he said.

Situ Rinpoché then removed from its special case the letter given to him by the previous Karmapa. After reading it, he queried the father. "What are the names of the parents? Are there clusters of juniper above and below the house? Is there a spring? Does the door of house face the west?"

"It's as you say," the father replied.

"Then keep all this secret for three months," Situ Rinpoché advised.

One month later, the great meditator Serphupa met the child and offered him his own damaru and bell. The child was delighted, played them, and gave everyone a blessing with his hand. Serphupa asked him, "If you're the Karmapa, tell me, what Dharma teaching did you give me at Tse Lhagang?"

"Mahāmudrā and the six yogas of Naropa," replied the young boy. In time, everyone came to believe that he was the incarnation of the Karmapa.

One Akhu Athar said, "If this is the Karmapa, deadly poison will not harm him." So he mixed poison with butter and rubbed it vigorously into the boy's body. It did not hurt him or have any negative effect.

Another person swore to the father, "If your child is the Karmapa, come what may, I will not receive his blessing." Later, when the Karmapa was giving a blessing with his hand to a huge crowd of people, he refrained from blessing this person who then developed faith and confessed his fault.

At this time in Draksum, a certain lama from Amdo had a son with some positive signs. He broadcast to everyone that his son was the Karmapa's reincarnation, and since he had courted almost everyone in the Great Encampment with material offerings, they supported him. Given this situation, although Gyaltsap Rinpoché knew that the reincarnation in Ngom was the true Karmapa, he had to pay some attention to what the people in the encampment thought, so he went to Draksum and met this son of the Amdo man. Gyaltsap Rinpoché offered three katas and all three were returned; not even one was kept. This inauspicious omen did not please Gyaltsap Rinpoché. Skilled in means, he made no statement about the child but just said that he should do some retreat in the temple at the top of his residence. When he was five, the Karmapa said, "This boy in Amdo is a reincarnation from Surmang. He's a monk of mine."

When the Karmapa was invited to the Great Encampment of Tsurphu, many special signs occurred: though it was winter, thunder, common to the summertime, clapped three times, and a cuckoo, a bird of the spring, sang three times. The members of the encampment finally admitted to Gyaltsap Rinpoché, "All you said was right." So, at the encampment, the Karmapa was placed on the lion throne during an auspicious ceremony.

When Mikyö Dorjé was seven, in front of the Jowo Gandhola, Gyaltsap Tashi Namgyal performed the hair-cutting ceremony, and the Karmapa received the signs of a renunciate, which included robes, and also the new name Chökyap Drakpa Pal Sangpo (All-Pervading Fame of the Dharma, Glorious and Excellent One). The Karmapa also received the Mahāyāna sojong vows for restoration and purification.

The king of Lower Yunnan repeatedly invited the Karmapa to visit. While Mikyö Dorjé was traveling there in 1516, thunder roared, a net of rainbows arched through the sky, and an elephant broke free of its rope and ran wild, so they had to search for it. Four military officers at the head of ten thousand soldiers came out to welcome the Karmapa, whose encampment was pitched in the vicinity of the king's palace. The following day at dawn, the king himself arrived at Gyamtri. He offered prostrations, and through the translator, Lakha Nyön, he inquired after the Karmapa's health and made offerings. An elephant also bowed and trumpeted loudly. Öthang Bum asked the mahout why the elephant had done this, and he replied, "He was so happy that the Buddha has come."

The Karmapa was invited to the palace and stayed for seven days, satisfying the king with the nectar of Dharma. The king vowed not to wage war against Tibet for thirteen years, and further, to build one hundred monasteries. Previously, this king did not respect the Buddha's teachings, but from that time onward he had unshakable faith in Buddhism in general and especially in the teachings of the Karma Kamtsang.

In accord with the previous Karmapa's prediction, when Mikyö Dorjé was ten, he took the great practitioner Sangyé Nyenpa from Denma as his main teacher and received novice vows from him. For another three years the Karmapa studied with Sangyé Nyenpa, receiving empowerments, reading transmissions, and commentary. Greatly pleased, the teacher said, "If I die, I'll have no regrets." And not long after, in 1519, Sangyé Nyenpa passed away into peace. The Karmapa then studied extensively with Dulmo Tashi Öser.

At the age of twenty-one, the Karmapa took full ordination with Pal Chödrup Sengé Shap as the abbot, Karma Trinlepa Chenpo as the ritual master, and Pal Shakya Sangpo as the private questioner. The Karmapa received many teachings from the abbot. With Karma Trinlepa he spent three sessions a day studying Haribhadra's commentary *Clarifying the Meaning*, which elucidates the *Ornament of Realization*. When the Karmapa asked for more sessions, they were increased so that he came to know the text completely in only two months. Afterward, he continued to study the other four Dharmas of Maitreya.

In the field of logic, Mikyö Dorjé studied Dignāga's *Compendium of Validity* along with its seven commentaries by Dharmakīrti. Three of them are the long, middle-length, and short commentaries that cover all the subjects of logic: the *Commentary on Validity*, the *Ascertainment of Validity*, and the *Drop of Reasoning*. Dharmakīrti's four other treatises, which are like secondary treatises, treat specific topics. Collectively, Dharmakīrti's seven works on Dignāga's single text are known as The Seven Treatises on Validity (or Valid Cognition).

Mikyö Dorjé further studied the *Compendium of Abhidharma* by Asaṅga (the higher Abhidharma) and the *Treasury of Abhidharma* by Vasubhandu (the lower Abhidharma), the root text of the *Vinaya Sutra* by Guṇaprabha, the *Fundamental Wisdom of the Middle Way* by Nāgārjuna, Candrakīrti's *Entering the Middle*

Way, *The Two Books* (on Hevajra), the *Compendium of Astrology*, and numerous other texts. In brief, in a three-year span, from age twenty-one to twenty-three, the Karmapa studied and easily comprehended the words and meaning of twenty-five major texts.

While Mikyö Dorjé was immersed in these texts, he did not even drink a cup of tea or notice if it was night or day. He contemplated the meaning of the words, cut through his doubts about difficult points, and refuted others' positions with reasoning and scripture, thereby bringing his knowledge to perfection. The Karmapa's teacher highly praised his diligence and wisdom.

Once, about halfway through the night, when Mikyö Dorjé had entered a nonconceptual state, his retinue thought that he had dissolved his body into the expanse of all phenomena and so they devoted themselves to long-life ceremonies. When Mikyö Dorjé returned from that state free of concepts, he gave many teachings on the Middle Way. "Now, thanks to this deep meaning," he said, "even if Ngok Lotsāwa, the Jonangpa (Dölpopa), Sakya Pandita, Butön, or Rongpo came to debate, I'd have no fear." From this time onward, the Karmapa fully comprehended the most subtle meaning found in the Prāsaṅgika, Svātantrika, and Shentong Madhyamaka traditions.

While Mikyö Dorjé was on the way to Changkyi Phuk, Shang Yudrakpa (also known as Lama Shang, 1123–93, founder of the Tsalpa Kagyü) appeared to him in a pure vision and gave him a blessing. Due to this, Mikyö Dorjé took as his philosophical position that in the end, the way the Prāsaṅgika postulates the Middle Way was excellent, so he composed the great commentary on *Entering the Middle Way* penetrating the meaning of the major Prāsaṅgika texts. He accepted Candrakīrti's presentation, but when it came to the ultimate, definitive meaning, Mikyö Dorjé stayed with the Shentong view, stemming from the thought of the Third Karmapa

Rangjung Dorjé. Mikyö Dorjé said that these difficult topics were not for ordinary individuals.

The Karmapa composed a great number of texts. From a young age he wrote numerous treatises and wonderful vajra songs. At twenty-two he composed an annotated commentary on the root text of the *Vinaya Sutra*. At twenty-three he wrote *The Noble One Resting at Ease*, a commentary on the Prajñāpāramitā literature. At twenty-five, he composed a great commentary on the *Kalāpa Grammar* (a Sanskrit grammar); at twenty-six, he authored an extensive commentary on the root text of the *Vinaya Sutra*; and at twenty-seven, he wrote his great commentary on the *Treasury of Abhidharma*. Finally, at thirty-nine he composed the extensive and profound *Chariot of the Dakpo Kagyü Siddhas*, which illuminates the philosophy of the Madhyamaka. In this way he created many important texts to provide gradual instruction on the various categories of Dharma in the sutra tradition, and he also composed commentaries on the tantras such as Mahāmāyā. His collected works contain some twenty volumes.

When Mikyö Dorjé was forty in 1546, he said, "I'm going to another pure realm," and so Shamar Rinpoché, Pawo Rinpoché, and others individually offered him long-life ceremonies, and he agreed to live another eight years. Finally, at the age of forty-eight, on the twenty-third of the eighth month in the year of the Wood Tiger from the ninth sixty-year cycle (1554), he withdrew the emanated mandala of his physical form and his mind entered the expanse of all phenomena.

His main disciples included the Fifth Shamar Könchok Yenlak, the Second Pawo Tsuklak Trengwa, the Third Gyaltsap Drakpa Paljor, the Fourth Situ Chökyi Gocha, and Ngotro Rabjam Namgyal.

1. The Ninth Karmapa Wangchuk Dorjé
2. Drölkar Yishin Khorlo
3. The Fifth Situ Chökyi Gyaltsen
4. The Third Pawo Tsuklak Gyatso
5. Yongzin Namgyal Drakpa
6. Attendants

The Ninth Karmapa Wangchuk Dorjé

1556–1603

According to the prediction of the previous Karmapa, the Ninth took rebirth in the country of lower Trehor. His father was Ador and his mother was Lingsa Alö. In her dreams she saw many positive signs: a golden mandala in her lap radiated lights; the sound of a resonating conch shell spread in every direction; and traveling through the sky, she encouraged many villagers to recite the six-syllable mantra of Avalokiteśvara. The father also had numerous dreams, such as a blue lion cub standing up in his lap. While the Karmapa was in his mother's womb, the local people witnessed many unusual things as well: in his parents' village, rainbow lights and sweet fragrances filled the air; everywhere, both inside and outside, the natural sound of the six-syllable mantra could be heard; and a variety of musical sounds could be perceived at different times.

Wangchuk Dorjé was born on the seventh day of the seventh month in the year of the Fire Dragon (1556). He immediately passed his hand over his face three times and declared with wide-open eyes, "I'm the Karmapa." His mother called him Namkha Gyalpo (King of Space).

At about four months old, when he held a thangka or other religious image in his hands, he would say, "OṂ ĀḤ HŪṂ," blessing it with his body, speech, and mind.

When he was asked for a dedication, he said, "May you attain full awakening." Everyone was amazed.

Later in the Karmapa's life, when Situ Chökyi Gocha was offering him the empowerment known as Tsewang Drup Gyalma, he had a vision of the Karmapa as White Amitābha. When the Karmapa offered the leftovers of his long-life pills to Situ Rinpoché, he experienced them as a hundred tastes he had not known before.

Another time, Situ Rinpoché offered the young boy the bell of the Seventh Karmapa, Chödrak Gyatso, asking, "Did this belong to Mikyö Dorjé or Chödrak Gyatso?" His answer came clearly, "Chödrak Gyatso."

A messenger from Shamar Rinpoché came to invite the Karmapa to the Great Encampment in Central Tibet. The messenger asked, "Would you have any words for Shamar Rinpoché?" The Karmapa replied, "He should come as quickly as possible. Has he no regard for me?"

A while later, the Karmapa said, "Today we'll hear a pleasant tale." The messenger then returned to the Karmapa and told stories of Shamar Rinpoché's travels around Drichu, which delighted the Karmapa. When Shamar Rinpoché and his entourage arrived, he prostrated to the Karmapa and paid him great respect. The Karmapa was invited to the encampment, known as the Ornament of the World, and formally placed on his great throne.

The young incarnation insisted that his hair-cutting ceremony take place quickly, and so in 1561 when the Karmapa was six years old, Shamar Rinpoché performed this ceremony in front of the Jowo Gandhola. He offered the Karmapa the name Palden Mipham Chökyi Wangchuk (Glorious, Unconquerable, Powerful One of the Dharma) as well as the five lay precepts and the bodhisattva vows.

Shamar Rinpoché became his teacher, and with him the Karmapa studied and contemplated the words of the Buddha, an ocean of sutras, tantras, and oral instructions along with empowerments and commentaries plus the collected works of previous Kagyü masters.

When he was eleven, the Karmapa took renunciate vows with Shamar Rinpoché as the abbot and Pawo Tsuklak Trengwa as the ritual master. He received the name Palden Mipham Chökyi Wangchuk Dorjé Garwang Choklé Nampar Gyalwai Nyingpo Khyapdak Tenpai Nyima (Glorious, Unconquerable, Powerful One of the Dharma, Compelling Vajra Dance, the Heart of Victory in All Directions, the All-Pervasive Lord, Sun of the Teachings).

From the Lord Pawo Tsuklak Trengwa, he received many empowerments and Dharma teachings, such as mahāmudrā and the six yogas. When the Karmapa was sixteen, from the first day of the New Year onward, he studied many texts in the sutra tradition, including the *Perfection of Wisdom*, Dharmakīrti's *Commentary on Validity*, and the *Treasury of Abhidharma*.

At the age of twenty-four, in the presence of the entire Sangha, he took vows of full ordination with the Fifth Shamar Könchok Yenlak as the abbot, Gyaltsap Drakpa Paljor as the ritual master, and Khawang Namgyal Drakpa as the private questioner.

Wangchuk Dorjé's writings, clear and profound, are still studied in monastic colleges. His compositions include treatises on dialectics such as the *Core Texts on Reasoning*; a commentary on Candrakīrti's *Entering the Middle Way* titled *A Feast for the Fortunate*; and a commentary on Abhidharma known as *Youthful Play*. He also composed manuals to bring about the realization of coemergent mahāmudrā: the longer *Ocean of Definitive Meaning*, the shorter *Eliminating the Darkness of Ignorance*, and the shortest, *Pointing Out the Dharmakāya*. His collected works consist of more than ten volumes, which are clearly noted in his spiritual biography.

When he was forty-eight, on the twenty-eighth day of the first month in the Water Hare year from the tenth cycle of sixty years (1603), at dawn amid wondrous signs and in the presence of followers clinging to permanence, he displayed how mind passes into the expanse of all phenomena.

His many disciples included the Sixth Shamar Chökyi Wangchuk, the reincarnation of Dakpo Tashi Namgyal, Jetsun Taranatha, the Fifth Situ Chökyi Gyaltsen, and the Third Pawo Tsuklak Gyatso.

1. The Tenth Karmapa Chöying Dorjé
2. Chenresik Chakshipa
3. The Fourth Pawo Tsuklak Kunsang
4. The Third Treho Tenzin Dargyé
5. Attendant Kuntu Sangpo

The Tenth Karmapa Chöying Dorjé

1604–74

In the lower part of Dokham (Amdo and Eastern Tibet), in an area of Rölchen Chogyé called Meröl (these days known as Gulok), the Tenth Karmapa was born as the youngest of three sons to his father, Khyeu Thar, and his mother, Atso. It was in 1604, the year of the Wood Dragon, on the twenty-third day of the third month in the tenth of the sixty-year cycles. As she was giving birth, his mother had a pure vision of Guru Padmasambhava (the Lotus-Born Teacher, also known as Guru Rinpoché of Ogyen), who gave a blessing, and so she named her son Ogyen Kyap (Protected by Ogyen).

From a young age the boy drew images of deities and made woven designs with yarns in various colors. Once, when he was carrying on his back a child named Tashi, the young incarnation turned a stalk of hollow grass into a reed to play and sang, "I'm the Karmapa. Play the gyaling well!" Based on this and other events, the news spread that the Karmapa had taken birth in the land of Gulok.

The Sixth Shamar Chökyi Wangchuk recognized the child as the Karmapa and sent his close personal assistant with an attendant to see him. Shamar Rinpoché gave the Karmapa the name Chöying Dorjé, which came from a terma of Guru Rinpoché. Chökyi Wangchuk also sent supplications for the Karmapa's long life evoking the power of truth so that all would go well for him. In 1611, Chökyi Wangchuk performed the hair-cutting ceremony. Subsequently the Karmapa was invited to the Great Encampment of Tsurphu, where he was formally installed on the lion throne.

When the Karmapa was twelve, in the presence of the Jowo Gandhola at Tsurphu, Pawo Tsuklak Gyatso performed the hair-cutting ceremony, trimming a tuft of hair from the Karmapa's head and giving him all the lay precepts. Afterward, beginning with a blessing empowerment of White Tārā, the Karmapa received from Pawo Rinpoché all the empowerments, reading transmissions, and commentaries that he needed, including teachings on the Kangyur, the tantras, key oral instructions, explanations of commentaries, and the collected writings of the previous Kagyü masters.

The Karmapa benefited others in many ways. To each of those who committed to stay in mountain retreat, he gave an image of Milarepa that he himself had created, and to each of those who committed to recite one hundred million manis, he gave an image he had fashioned of Avalokiteśvara. Chöying Dorjé inspired almost all of the lay people to take a vow not to kill. He refused invitations to banquets where meat and alcohol were served and did not give them to others.

At the age of twenty-one, he took full ordination with Shamar Rinpoché acting as the abbot, Pawo Tsuklak Gyatso as the ritual master, and Situ Chökyi Gyaltsen as the private questioner.

To benefit others, he traveled to Lhasa, Namtso, Sakya, Chubar, and many other places. One day a letter arrived from Lhodrak, saying that Pawo Rinpoché had entered into peace, and not long after Shamar Rinpoché also dissolved his mind into the expanse of all phenomena. Treho Rinpoché then became the Karmapa's close attendant.

When he arrived in Lhasa, the Karmapa did one hundred thousand outer and one hundred thousand inner circumambulations of each of the two main statues in

Lhasa: the Jowo Mikyö Dorjé (a statue of the eight-year old Śākyamuni) and Jowo Śākyamuni (the Buddha at twelve years). The Karmapa offered to the Jowo Śākyamuni a scarf of the finest silk about fifteen feet long and five feet wide. The next day the Karmapa received it back from him; tied in three auspicious knots, it was placed around the Karmapa's neck. Through Chöying Dorjé's activity, the devotion of the faithful for the two Jowo statues increased, and they were inspired to engage in positive actions, such as prostrating and circumambulating.

Then one time, Mongolian soldiers and people from Lhasa surrounded the Great Encampment, so the Karmapa and his attendant Kuntu Sangpo were forced to leave. While they were traveling to Khenpa Jong, some of the soldiers in pursuit saw them as deer, while others saw them as vultures. The soldiers chased the two men but could not catch them, and their armies destroyed the Great Encampment.

During most of the escape, the Karmapa and his attendant also appeared to others in a variety of ways: some thought that the Karmapa and five disciples had traveled to Samyé, and others that he had gone to Lhasa or Kongpo Götsang. The army searched again and again but could not find them. As the Lord of Dharma and Kuntu Sangpo walked to Khenpa Jong, they had no warm clothes or food for twelve days, but Guru Rinpoché provided them with nectar, so they were neither cold nor hungry.

For three years Kuntu Sangpo served as the Karmapa's attendant, not letting his care slacken for a moment; all told, he continuously served the Karmapa for thirty-five years. Later, the Karmapa gave him a high rank and valued him greatly. When material offerings were made to the Karmapa, he immediately gave them to Kuntu Sangpo.

In 1647 the king of Jang Satham (or Lijiang, a kingdom in the far south of Eastern Tibet) sent an invitation, which the Karmapa accepted. Escorting him to his palace, the king made extensive offerings, including the eight auspicious symbols and the seven articles of royalty all fashioned in gold. Every high-ranking official invited the Karmapa to their residences and showed him great respect. In turn, he satisfied them all with the nectar of Dharma.

Then, knowing that the reincarnation of Shamar had taken birth, the Karmapa wanted to recognize him and invite him to the Great Encampment. So he gave his personal belongings to his attendant Kuntu Sangpo, and disguised as a mendicant, the Karmapa loaded up a horse with what he might need. As he traveled alone to the country of Gulok, a band of bandits stole his horse, his clothes—everything he had. Barefoot like a beggar, the Karmapa continued on his way even as his feet became frostbitten and covered with sores. Since he had no cup or clothes, one person offered him a bowl that was pieced together from five parts, and another gave his warm felt garment to the Karmapa, who used both of these gifts. A householder gave him food until the sores on his feet healed.

As he continued on his journey, the Karmapa was recognized, so many people came to meet him. Knowing of the Karmapa's coming, the young Shamar traveled out to welcome him. During the hair-cutting ceremony, the Karmapa gave him the name Yeshé Nyingpo (Heart of Wisdom).

When Chöying Dorjé went to the Potala Palace, he met the Fifth Dalai Lama, who inquired about the Karmapa's travels and asked him numerous questions about the Dharma. Since the Karmapa was advanced in years, it was difficult for him to hear at a distance, so Kuntu Sangpo relayed their words back and forth. Great banquets and excellent gifts were offered to the Karmapa. When he came into the presence of the Buddha statue known as the Jowo, infinite pure visions arose. He also remembered a previous incarnation as the king Songtsen Gampo, who had dissolved into the Jowo's heart.

Not long afterward, in 1674, corresponding to the year of the Wood Tiger in the eleventh sixty-year cycle, at dawn on the fifteenth day of the second month, when he was seventy-one, the Karmapa's mind departed for the expanse of all phenomena. His precious remains were brought to Tsurphu.

His main students were the Seventh Shamar Yeshé Nyingpo, Taklung Shapdrung Tashi Paldrup, the attendant Kuntu Sangpo, the Sixth Situ Chögyal Mipham Trinlé (also known as Mipham Trinlé Rabten), the Sixth Gyaltsap Norbu Sangpo, the Fourth Pawo Tsuklak Kunsang, Khedrup Raga Asya (Karma Chakmé), and Rinchen Jatsön Nyingpo.

1. The Eleventh Karmapa Yeshé Dorjé
2. Dorjé Phakmo
3. Yongey Mingyur Dorjé
4. Treho Karma Guru Thuchen Tsal

The Eleventh Karmapa Yeshé Dorjé

1676–1702

Yeshé Dorjé was born in the area of Markham in 1676, the year of the Fire Male Dragon. The Seventh Shamar Yeshé Nyingpo and the Sixth Gyaltsap Norbu Sangpo invited him to Central Tibet. As they traveled, the young incarnation matured the Dharma practice of everyone he met. Escorted by a resplendent procession of monks, he came to the unsurpassed palace of Tsurphu. During a positive conjunction of the planets and stars, the Karmapa was formally placed on the lion throne, and good wishes were offered for everything to be auspicious.

The Karmapa received from Shamar Rinpoché empowerments, reading transmissions, and commentaries belonging to his own tradition, which included mahāmudrā and the six yogas. From the vajra speech of Guru Padmasambhava, who gave a list of names for the Karmapas in a terma, he received the name Yeshé Dorjé. He also mastered listening and reflecting on the empowerments, reading transmissions, and key instructions of the Nyingma tradition. Yeshé Dorjé had many spiritual friends as his teachers, such as the Third Karma Trinlepa and the Sixth Gyaltsap Norbu Sangpo, so he studied widely the empowerments, reading transmissions, and key instructions found in both the sutras and tantras. In 1694, when the Seventh Shamar entered into peace, the Karmapa created many offerings for the funeral service and new representations of body, speech, and mind.

The Fifth Dalai Lama treated with special favor Treho Rinpoché Karma Tenzin Dargyé and appointed him as an attendant. In 1682, the Dalai Lama passed away, and the Dharma king Desi Sangyé Gyatso said that he needed Treho Rinpoché to remain as his main lama. Later, in 1690, Treho Rinpoché was released from his position and went to Tsurphu. There he met the Karmapa, and they talked about everything under the sun. When Gyaltsap Rinpoché and Pawo Rinpoché passed away, the Karmapa performed their funeral services one after the other.

In 1695, the Eighth Shamar took birth in Nepal and spoke many times about his memories of previous lives as the incarnation of Shamar. On a piece of paper the Karmapa drew the layout of the place where Shamar's reincarnation was born. Entrusting it into the hands of messengers, he charged them to find the reincarnation. They were able to recognize as the unmistaken reincarnation the young boy found in Nepal's Yölmo Gangi Rawa. In order to pry him loose from the control of the Nepalese king Mantra Singha Malla, Desi Sangyé Gyatso granted the request of the Karmapa and sent to Nepal both a powerful emissary who had connections in the country, and also the treasurer from the central government. In 1700, the young incarnation was invited from Nepal and brought to Tibet. Treho Rinpoché made all the arrangements for the outer preparations around the monastery and also for the inner ones in the Karmapa's quarters. Finally, the reincarnation arrived at Tsurphu.

The Karmapa performed the hair-cutting ceremony and gave the incarnation a new name. The Karmapa was offered long-life prayers, a hanging with a double vajra design for the front of a throne, and many other articles. Wearing the red crown of the Shamar, the incarnation was formally placed on the lion throne.

The reincarnation of Situ Chögyal Mipham was born as the son of Gön Lhünpo, head of the Ling family. The Karmapa recognized the Situpa and gave him a name.

The family, however, followed its own wishes, placing him in the Sakya lineage, and so the tulku died at a very young age. His reincarnation was the Eighth Situ Kunkhyen Chökyi Jungné. The Karmapa had laid out a new astrological diagram for making predictions, and this indicated that Situ Rinpoché would be born in the year of the Iron Dragon in the Alo family. After a special child was born to him, Alo Kunkhyen sent a message with Khamnyön Tulku, who went to Central Tibet and met the Karmapa at Tsurphu. When the Karmapa heard the words of Alo Kunkhyen about his child, the sun shone and many auspicious connections came together. The Karmapa said, "Now the auspicious connections are most excellent. Situ Rinpoché has been born in Dergé." The Karmapa had already known about the reincarnation and had written a formal statement of recognition, which he gave to Khamnyön Tulku. The Sixth Pawo Rinpoché Tsuklak Döndrup and many others also recognized this reincarnation of Situ Rinpoché, who benefited many people from all walks of life—high, low, and in between. For example Gyurmé Namgyal, the great practitioner from Dengri, was blind in both eyes. He rubbed them with Situ Rinpoché's saliva and immediately could see clearly.

At the end of his life, the Karmapa appointed Shamar Palchen Chökyi Döndrup as his regent and entrusted him with the essential matters related to preserving the Karmapa's teachings. After prophesying where he would take birth, Yeshé Dorjé withdrew the display of his incarnation to encourage the Dharma practice of his disciples who were attached to permanence. It was 1702, when the Karmapa was twenty-seven years old, the year of the Water Horse in the twelfth sixty-year cycle on the twelfth day of the seventh month.

Among the Karmapa's many disciples, the main ones included the Eighth Shamar Palchen Chökyi Döndrup, Treho Karma Tenzin Dargyé, and Khenchen Karma Dönyö Nyingpo.

1. The Twelfth Karmapa Jangchup Dorjé
2. Tsasum Drildrup
3. Yongey Mingyur Dorjé
4. Terchen Chöjé Lingpa
5. The Seventh Pawo Tsuklak Gawa
6. Kharnak Dorjé Gyalpo

The Twelfth Karmapa Jangchup Dorjé

1703–32

During the year of the Water Female Sheep (corresponding to 1703) in the territory of Dergé in Dokham, Jangchup Dorjé was born to his father, Karma Tseten, and his mother, Karmo Kyi. The family lineage descended from the Tibetan Dharma kings, and their male lineage was the same as Karma Pakṣi's.

A certain Lama Dulwa offered the young boy a traditional ritual cleansing, and later this lama's eyes suffered a virulent infection. When he asked the treasure-finder Mingyur Dorjé what might help him to heal, Mingyur Dorjé replied, "You offered a ritual cleansing to the Gyalwang Karmapa, and this angered Palden Lhamo. That's the cause of your illness." That is how Mingyur Dorjé recognized the Karmapa.

Later, the liaison secretary of the encampment was sent from Central Tibet to Lhathok to meet with Mingyur Dorjé and talk about recognizing the Karmapa's reincarnation. The secretary was given the name of the region where the supreme reincarnation resided and the names of his father and mother. Based on this information, the secretary met with the reincarnation, who was able to recognize the previous Karmapa's statue, mala, and blessing cord knotted in the shape of a ritual dagger. Later, the Karmapa met Situ Chökyi Jungné and Dergé Lama along with many others. Following this, numerous tulkus came to meet the Karmapa, including Tralek Nyima Dorjé, Surmang Garwang, and Sangyé Nyenpa.

At the blossoming of the New Year of the Hare (1711), when he was nine years old, the Karmapa was invited by Situ Rinpoché and traveled to Alo Paljor Monastery. Situ Rinpoché asked him, "Who is my supreme deity? And who are my protectors?" "Tamdrin and Shingkyong," the young boy correctly replied. In 1712, messengers from Central Tibet arrived carrying an invitation, and so the Karmapa departed for Tsurphu with Situ Rinpoché, stopping on the way at Karma Gön. While he traveled along in stages, the Karmapa made meaningful connections with everyone who met him.

As they approached Tsurphu, the Eighth Shamar Chökyi Döndrup rode out to greet them, and the master (the Karmapa) and two disciples (Situ and Shamar Rinpochés) met at the place called Badrom Shung. Gradually they proceeded to Tsurphu accompanied by a resplendent procession of the Sangha. The Karmapa formally took his place on the golden throne and wore the luminous Black Crown. Garwang Rinpoché gave him his first Dharma teachings, which included reading transmissions for *Reciting the Names of Mañjuśrī* and the *Spontaneous Accomplishment of Wishes*. His first empowerment was the union of Amitāyus and Hayagrīva from the tradition of the siddha Thangtong Gyalpo. Subsequently his extensive studies encompassed the sutras, tantras, and key instructions as expounded by the victorious Kagyü and other lineages; the treatises of Indian and Tibetan scholars and meditation masters; the collected works of many great masters; and the empowerments, reading transmissions, and commentaries from the old and new traditions. Able to transform his dreams, the Karmapa traveled to Shambhala where he received the Kālacakra empowerment from the Kalki (Rikden) king.

In 1718, the Seventh Gyaltsap Könchok Öser offered the Karmapa the hair-cutting ceremony. At Tsurphu he met with Kathok Rikzin Chenpo, who gave him novice vows and teachings on mahāmudrā, the six yogas, and other practices.

During his twenty-first year, the Karmapa traveled with his heart sons Situ, Gyaltsap, and Shamar Rinpochés over the high mountains to Nepal. There the king of Yambu came out to greet them and offered a silken sedan. The king Jagajaya Malla (1722–35, twelfth of the Malla dynasty) rode out on an elephant accompanied by divisions of his army with their colorful banners fluttering and music filling the air. The king invited the Tibetans to his palace, where he arranged an immense banquet with a variety of dishes and fruits and also made extensive offerings of silver and gold flowers along with other precious objects. At this time, the king requested the Karmapa to halt a summertime disease that had turned into a raging epidemic no one had been able to stop for years. In Nepal there was a naturally arisen statue of Avalokiteśvara, one of five Nepali statues of him that were considered to be companions (as they came from the same sandalwood tree) and to possess great blessing. For a few days, the Karmapa turned his mind to this image and offered ritual purifications.

Then he and his three heart sons rode an elephant out to Yangleshö, a place of pilgrimage with caves where Guru Rinpoché had practiced. Here they engaged in the reversal practices of Dorjé Trolö (a wrathful form of Guru Rinpoché) and the protector Trakshé, and also performed fire pujas. With the Karmapa and Shamar Rinpoché mounted on an elephant and Situ Rinpoché and Gyaltsap Rinpoché on fine stallions, they rode around the perimeter of the city dispensing the purifying water. This brought the epidemic to an end, and the city was able to grow again. The king, his ministers, and the people of Nepal made generous offerings to the Karmapa, and he bestowed upon everyone the seed of rebirth in the higher realms and ultimate liberation.

The Karmapa and his heart sons went on pilgrimage to the three main stupas in Nepal: the supreme place of Namo Buddha (in Tibetan, Takmo Lujin, Generously

Offering His Body to the Tigress), Boudhanath, and Swayambhunath. They also went to a cave in the Kataya Mountains of Nyishang and, among many wonderful things, saw the footprint left by Lord Milarepa. After making numerous prostrations and aspiration prayers, the great lamas gradually made their way to Mount Kailash and other pilgrimage sites in Tibet. When they came to Samyé, the oracle Tsimar came out to welcome them at the Pehar Temple known as Korzö Ling, and they also met the oracle Pehar in his temple. Pehar drank the Karmapa's saliva and promised to engage in Dharma activity. The Karmapa instructed him, "Not harming living beings—that in itself is Dharma activity."

Later, traveling through Nepal, they came to Kushinagara in India. Then at Surmang and other places, the Karmapa gave renunciate vows to the reincarnations of Rölpa Dorjé, Mingyur Dorjé, and Rechungpa plus two hundred other people. He gave full ordination to the reincarnation of Garwang Rinpoché along with two hundred other monks. Afterward, he bestowed full ordination on Situ Rinpoché's nephew, Karma Tsaptsa Lama, together with one hundred other Sangha members.

The fourth Dharma king of Sikkim, Gyurmé Namgyal, traveled to Tsurphu disguised as a servant. Aware of this, the Karmapa set up a great throne and created an extensive welcome for the ruler. Jangchup Dorjé made splendid offerings to this Dharma king, who promised to found a new monastery for the Karmapa. True to his word, the king built Phodong Rabten Ling Monastery in Sikkim. Without impediment, the Karmapa consecrated it from afar, and the grains that fell there can be seen at the monastery.

A golden letter of invitation came twice from the palace of the emperor of China, so the Karmapa entrusted the heart essence of the teachings to Situ Chökyi Jungné and gave him copious advice on how to maintain the teachings of the Karma Kamtsang tradition. Then the Karmapa and Shamar Rinpoché left for China. On the thirtieth day of the tenth month in the Water Mouse Year as the sun rose in China, the Karmapa withdrew the mandala of his temporary manifestation into the expanse of all phenomena. The next month, the Eighth Shamar also manifested the way of flowing into the expanse of all phenomena.

The Karmapa's attendants, the secretary Surri, and others cremated the precious remains and brought the ashes and bone relics to Tsurphu. Situ Rinpoché and Gyaltsap Rinpoché consecrated them in front of the great Buddha statue known as the Ornament of the World, and two silver-encased reliquary stupas were built, one for the Gyalwang Karmapa and one for Shamar Rinpoché.

Jangchup Dorjé's main students included Situ Chökyi Jungné, whom the Karmapa appointed the holder of his teachings and his regent; Kagyü Trinlé Shingta, the supreme, omniscient reincarnation of the Drukpa Kagyü; both the Sixth Pawo Tsuklak Döndrup and the Seventh Pawo Tsuklak Gawa; Kathok Rikzin Tsewang Norbu; the Seventh Gyaltsap Könchok Öser; Treho Chöjé; and the Karmapa's teacher Karma Thupten.

1. The Thirteenth Karmapa Düdul Dorjé
2. Kagyü Trinlé Shingta
3. Tsuktor Dukar
4. Kagyü Trinlé Namgyal
5. Karma Düdul Gyalpo
6. Attendant
7. Tsepakmé
8. Gurgyi Gönpo

The Thirteenth Karmapa Düdul Dorjé

1733–97

As prophesied by the previous Karmapa and others, his next incarnation was born in Nyen Tsawa Drong, located in a southern district of Central Tibet. This was during the waxing moon of the eighth month in the year of the Water Female Ox from the twelfth sixty-year cycle (1733). Since he recounted many memories from previous lives, people had complete certainty, free of any doubt, that he was the supreme incarnation, and his fame spread everywhere. The infant had a red birthmark at his heart and a naturally arisen letter A on his tongue.

In 1736 a group led by the Seventh Gyaltsap Könchok Öser along with the former head of provisions, the master of the chambers, and the liaison secretary went out to welcome the reincarnation, and the young boy seemed very pleased. A brilliant procession in great pageantry escorted him to Okmin Tsurphu. In the presence of the Dalai Lama Thamché Khyenpa Kalsang Gyatso and the Karmapa's heart sons, the Karmapa was installed on the great lion throne and given his formal name. He wore the crown offered by one hundred thousand ḍākiṇīs and made meaningful connections with all who met him.

The Eighth Tai Situpa Tenpai Nyinché traveled from the Dergé area of Domé to Tsurphu in 1745, and there the Karmapa (as the young master) and Tai Situpa (as the older disciple) met. On the fifteenth day of the auspicious fourth Tibetan month, in the presence of the Buddha statue known as the Ornament of the World, the Karmapa received both the lay precepts and novice vows from Situ Rinpoché. In addition, the Karmapa studied the sutras and tantras with him and received empowerments, reading transmissions, and commentaries from the old and new schools. The Karmapa received these profound and vast teachings like water being poured from one vessel into another. In this way Situ Rinpoché became his root teacher or Lord of the Family. The Karmapa also studied widely with other learned and realized teachers, such as Rikzin Tsewang Norbu, Kagyü Trinlé Shingta, and the Seventh Pawo Tsuklak Gawa.

With Situ Rinpoché acting as the abbot and Pawo Tsuklak Gawa as the ritual master, the Karmapa took full ordination in the presence of a full complement of authentic, fully ordained monks. The Karmapa also received multiple oral instructions and profound commentaries on texts such as the six yogas of Naropa.

At one time, floods arose at the Jokhang, Lhasa's central temple, and no matter what was done to stop them, nothing worked. So following a prediction of Guru Rinpoché, the central government invited the Karmapa to Lhasa. He first chanted the *Seven-Branch Offering*, and then as soon as he recited the supplication known as *Reversing the Approach of the Serpent*, the waters receded.

When he was thirty-nine years old, Düdul Dorjé traveled toward Dergé and the Amdo area to met with Tai Situ Tenpai Nyinché, who offered him teachings on the Madhyamaka view. The Karmapa reciprocated by offering his mastery of resting in meditation throughout the day and night. When he journeyed to Palpung, the Karmapa made meaningful connections with everyone he met along the way, and then by stages returned to Tsurphu.

Having realized the nature of dirt and gold to be the same, he saw all the phenomena of samsara and nirvana like illusions or dreams, and he was not affected by any of the eight worldly concerns. When beggars made requests, he gave them the clothes off his back and the blessing cords from around his neck. When blind beggars, the destitute, and the unfortunate whom others scorned and spurned came to him, the Karmapa gazed at them with loving eyes and placed within their minds the seed of liberation. He did this through various skillful means, such as pleasing conversation that was playful and full of stories about amazing experiences. When the blind and other beggars fought among themselves, the Karmapa reconciled them with his advice. He was also very patient. If he would explain to someone who was not so bright that all phenomena were like an illusion, and this person were to astonish him by taking "illusion" (*sgyu ma*) to mean "intestines" (*rgyu ma*), the Karmapa would still try in many ways to plant the seed of virtue in that person's mind.

Once a rabbit came before him to request the Dharma. While the Karmapa told a brief story related to the Dharma, the rabbit sat with its eyes wide open and its paws joined together in front of its body. After the Karmapa had given it meditation instruction, the rabbit's mind came to rest in stability. On the third day, the rabbit offered the Karmapa three blades of grass as a mandala. There are numerous such incredible stories about how the Karmapa guided all living beings onto the path of liberation and omniscience, no matter what their level might be.

At the end of his life, Düdul Dorjé entrusted his teachings to the Ninth Situ Rinpoché Pema Nyinché Wangpo and also bequeathed a prediction letter, which the Karmapa had signed and sealed. It foretold the country where he would come in the future, the names of his parents, and other details. Until that time he appointed Jepön Karma Paldrup as his regent and then gave his close disciples copious advice. Finally, to inspire the Dharma practice of those who clung to permanence, at the age of sixty-five on the twenty-fourth day of the first month of the year of the Fire

Snake from the thirteenth sixty-year cycle (1797), Düdul Dorjé demonstrated how the reflection of an emanation body is withdrawn.

His main disciples included the Ninth Situ Pema Nyinché Wangpo, Drukchen Kunsik Chökyi Nangwa, the Eighth Pawo Tsuklak Chögyal, Rikzin Dorjé Drakpo, the nephews Jeön Döndrup Tulku and Jeön Chöwang Tulku from Palpung, and Kadra Nyen Tulku. Also among the Karmapa's disciples were many powerful scholars and practitioners who made the Kagyü teachings flourish like the waxing moon.

1. The Fourteenth Karmapa Thekchok Dorjé
2. Tseringma
3. Khorwa Dongtruk
4. Jeön Döndrup Tulku
5. Jeön Chöwang Tulku

The Fourteenth Karmapa Thekchok Dorjé

1797–1868

As predicted by the previous Karmapa, in a place called Danang Yilung Tashi Thongmön, belonging to Eastern Tibet's Salmo Gang, the Fourteenth Karmapa was born to his father, Gönpo Lha, and his mother, Sönam Lhamo. The birth occurred during the daytime on the twelfth day of the twelfth month in the year of the Fire Snake from the thirteenth sixty-year cycle (1797). Before the Karmapa's birth, his mother dreamt that she met the previous Karmapa Düdul Dorjé, who was wearing the Black Crown and sitting on a golden throne in what seemed to be a shrine hall at Tsurphu. The mother offered prostrations and requested a blessing, which the Karmapa gave her with great joy. She awoke to the experience of limitless happiness. During the pregnancy and birth, there were many amazing signs. During the twelfth month in the winter, for example, brilliant flowers blossomed in a small garden just an armspan square.

As soon as he came into the world, the newborn sat up straight and repeated the Sanskrit alphabet with an intense gaze. When Drukchen Chökyi Nangwa became certain that the circumstances of this infant accorded with the prediction left by the previous Karmapa, he recognized the child as the Karmapa and gave him the name Palden Rigkun Lhundrup Thekpa Chogi Dorjé Ngedön Tenpai Nyima Choklé Namgyal Kuntu Gawa Gyepaidé, (Glorious Spontaneous Presence of All the Buddha Families, Vajra of the Supreme Vehicle, Sun of the Teachings of the Definitive Meaning, Victorious in All Directions, Joy Spreading Everywhere).

At Karma Gön (the Karmapa's monastery in Eastern Tibet), Thekchok Dorjé received lay precepts and novice vows from the Ninth Situ Pema Nyinché Wangpo in the presence of a statue of the First Karmapa Düsum Khyenpa that was known to speak. The young Karmapa then studied the profound and vast teachings that mature and liberate, which are found in the Secret Mantrayāna of both the old and new traditions. Then he made his way by stages to Tsurphu, where he took full ordination with Drukchen Chökyi Nangwa serving as the abbot and Situ Rinpoché as the ritual master.

The young Karmapa studied extensively with many teachers who were scholars and masters of meditation. He excelled in all the arts, such as painting deities, sculpting, metal casting, and sewing appliqué images. The wisdom of his lively mind penetrated into broad areas of study that encompassed astrology, grammar, poetry, the stylistics of composition, and agriculture. In particular he favored the study of the inner sciences of the mind, focusing on the Tripiṭaka and other important texts.

During the specially blessed time of the fourth Tibetan month known as Saga Dawa, the Karmapa instituted the practice of the Eighth Chapter of the *Guhyasamāja* on the tenth day of the month and also the longer, intensive practice of Vajrakīlaya along with lama dancing.

Once Thekchok Dorjé went together with the Great Encampment to Damshung. While he was wearing the Black Crown and bestowing the Dharma, a few people saw that from the peak of a mountain inhabited by nonhuman spirits called tsengö, a few had come to serve the Karmapa, and he was binding them under oath.

Another time, when the Karmapa was residing at the edge of a lake, some saw that he had pitched a blue tent in the middle of the lake, where he stayed for seven days. Others among the faithful saw him as a young man, and some as old. Each of the disciples had their own way of seeing him.

On another occasion, the Karmapa was standing before the face of a steep mountain where malevolent spirits were known to live. Suddenly, a huge boulder along with many smaller stones the size of a goat's head descended in a rumbling avalanche. Terrified, the entire entourage ran about in a frenzy, calling out "*Karmapa khyenno*!" ("Karmapa, know me!") With a mere glance, the Karmapa stopped the boulder in midflight down the precipitous mountainside, and the other stones vanished into some faraway, unknown place. Many such incredible events happened around the Karmapa as signs of his realization.

While he was practicing the *Sādhana of the Three Roots Combined*, a terma of Chokgyur Lingpa, there clearly appeared a long-life arrow with silken streamers, which was three finger-widths wide. Such special signs along with other indications revealed that the Karmapa had attained the level of a vidyādhara with power over his lifespan. However, in order to work with disciples who were attached to permanence, the Karmapa confirmed that he would reveal his final deed and also spoke of many other things.

Although his main disciples, imbued with intense devotion, made supplications for his long life, in the end the Karmapa entrusted Drukchen Rinpoché with what was essential to preserving the Karmapa's teachings and empowered him as the regent. In particular, the Karmapa entrusted the precious teachings of Tsurphu to his two nephews who were reincarnate lamas, Chöwang Tulku and Döndrup Tulku. He also advised that the remains of his body should not be cremated but placed in their entirety within a stupa. On the twenty-first day of the first month in the year of the Earth Dragon from the fifteenth sixty-year cycle (1868), Thekchok Dorjé withdrew the manifestation of his physical form.

His main disciples were Drukchen Jikmé Mingyur Wangyal, Jamgön Kongtrul Yönten Gyatso, Tertön Chokgyur Lingpa, Jamyang Khyentsé Wangpo, the Tenth Situ Pema Kunsang, the Ninth Gyaltsap Yeshé Sangpo, the Ninth Pawo Tsuklak Nyinché, and the two nephews Jeön Chöwang Tulku and Jeön Döndrup Tulku. Like the sun and moon, Thekchok Dorjé's many disciples illuminated the teachings.

1. The Fifteenth Karmapa Khakhyap Dorjé
2. Gönpo Shaljor
3. Gyalwa Gyatso Yabyum
4. Khyentsé Shenphen Dorjé
5. Karma Ngedön Tengyé

The Fifteenth Karmapa Khakhyap Dorjé

1871–1922

Khakhyap Dorjé was born to his father, the tantric practitioner Ketong Drupchen Nyendrak Wangpo (who was the most important of five brothers) and to his mother, Kalsang Drölma, in the district of Tsang in Central Tibet. It was on the tenth day of the eighth month in the year of the Iron Sheep from the fifteenth cycle of sixty years (1871). As soon as he was born, he looked vividly into space; this and many other special signs occurred. His parents gave him the name Döndrup Dorjé (Vajra Achieving Benefits).

At one time, the child was invited to attend lama dances at Tsechen Monastery. As he was traveling there, dusk was approaching, and below the road on a riverbank there appeared a few begging monks dressed in rags and carrying a load on their backs. Above the road in a curved hollow, a flock of black birds had gathered and were raising a ruckus. As the travelers moved a little further down the road, the night so enveloped them they could not see anything. Then a great fire, blazing fiercely in blue and red, came after them. Thinking it was a ghost, people were terrified and repeatedly took refuge in the Buddha, Dharma, and Sangha. Powerless to do anything, they escaped anywhere they could. But the Karmapa did not show even the slightest fear; he merely turned a loving gaze toward the fire. Without doing any harm it dispersed like a field of stars, growing smaller and smaller and vanishing into the dark.

In harmony with the wisdom vision of Jamyang Khyentsé Wangpo, Jamgön Kongtrul Lodrö Thayé, and Chokgyur Dechen Lingpa plus the Ninth Pawo Tsuklak Nyinché and others, Drukchen Rinpoché recognized the Karmapa at the age of six by clearly revealing the country where the reincarnation lived, the details of his house, his family lineage and clan, and his father.

In 1877, Döndrup Tulku (a nephew of the previous Karmapa) and his disciples offered the young incarnation robes along with a new name and invited him to Tsurphu. In the early part of the morning on the eighth day of the fourth month, a victory banner was placed on top of the Karmapa's birthplace. A smoke offering was made, a ritual cleansing was offered to the young boy, and special food was prepared. The sun shone and a mixture of snow and rain fell as summer thunder rolled through the sky. The many auspicious signs were wondrous.

On the third day of the fifth Tibetan month, Drukchen Rinpoché, Chöwang Rinpoché (the previous Karmapa's second nephew), Jang Drungpa Tulku, and others invited the Karmapa to his main seat of Tsurphu with an impressive procession of lamas and tulkus. He was formally installed on his golden throne and given the name Palden Kunsang Chökyi Nyima Chenpo Trinlé Khakhyap Dorjé Choklé Nampar Gyalwai Dé (Glorious All-Good, Great Sun of the Dharma, All-Pervading Vajra of Activity, Victorious in All Directions).

On the second day of the following month, the Karmapa took the vows of full ordination with Drukchen Rinpoché as the abbot, Dechen Yongzin Sheja Kunkhyen as the ritual master, and Lhenchen Rinchen Dargyé as the timekeeper. The two tulkus who were nephews made up the full complement of monks.

Afterward the Karmapa began to study. He memorized texts from the tantras and other books and learned to write various alphabets, such as uchen, umé, lentsa, wartu, and drutsa, mastering them down to the smallest curve. Throughout his whole life, he did not miss any of the regularly performed rituals on the tenth and fifteenth days of the waxing moon or on the eighteenth day or the twenty-ninth Mahākāla day of the waning moon. On the days between these ceremonies, there was no time for distraction as the Karmapa studied and contemplated extensively the commentaries on the great texts and the various sciences. From Khenchen Lama Tashi Öser he received reading transmissions for the Kangyur and the complete writings of the Nyingma master Tselé Natsok Rangdröl. From Pawo Tsuklak Nyinché he received the reading transmission and empowerments for the six volumes of texts composed by Jatsön Nyingpo. And from Ngakdra Rikzin Chenpo the Karmapa received the reading transmission for the complete writings of Situ Chökyi Jungné.

When he was fourteen, Khakhyap Dorjé completed the restoration and expansion of Pangpuk Monastery in Lithang. While a date for the consecration was being discussed, the Karmapa was asked to display a special sign, which he agreed to do. When the assigned day came, he was staying in a room underneath the curved roof of the shrine hall that sheltered the great image of the Buddha at Tsurphu. The Karmapa drew a picture of Pangpuk Monastery on a piece of paper and playfully tossed on this image some white rice that had been soaked in saffron water. At that same time, in Pangpuk Monastery, when everyone was saying, "Today a special sign will come," from the midst of a white cloud a rain of golden rice fell everywhere both inside and outside. All who were present witnessed it, and this golden rain gave them unshakable faith in the Karmapa.

Afterward, he traveled to Palpung and met Jamgön Kongtrul Lodrö Thayé. From him the Karmapa received general teachings on the Three Roots according to the Kagyü tradition and also the empowerments, reading transmissions, and commentaries for Jamgön Kongtrul's *Treasury of Kagyü Mantras* and other texts.

Once the Karmapa was encouraged by certain signs to compose a text of melodies that were chanted in order to remind Mahākāla and Mahākālī of their previous vows. At the break of dawn, the Karmapa dreamt that a dark-colored man holding a knife said to him, "It's good to compose a melody for me. This is the one that Thongwa Dönden (the Sixth Karmapa) wrote. Creating one like this is fine." Then he handed the Karmapa a brown scroll on which a melody was drawn. Immediately upon waking, he wrote down exactly what had appeared in his mind.

In 1888, on the twenty-seventh day of the first Tibetan month, the Karmapa departed for Palpung's upper retreat, the residence of Jamgön Kongtrul Rinpoché, who gave him the empowerments, reading transmissions, and commentaries from the *Treasury of Precious Termas*. The Karmapa also received explanations and commentaries on the view of the Madhyamaka, the Prajñāpāramitā sutras, and the Abhidharma as well as the *Supreme Continuum*, the *Root Tantra of Cakrasaṃvara*, the *Guhyasamāja Tantra*, *Stainless Light* (a commentary on the Kālacakra), and the *Guhyagarbha Tantra*. In addition, he received teachings on the sciences such as grammar, astrology, medicine, and the art of poetry.

At one time when the outer elements were not in balance and the inner winds were not entering their natural places, the Karmapa was very sick and nearing death. Then, following a prophecy of a dākiṇī from Ogyen, he was encouraged to take a consort, and this released him from the obstacles.

Another time, when Khakhyap Dorjé was in the protector shrine reciting the mantra of his radiant black yidam Mahākāla, there was a terrific cracking sound, tsak! The Mahākāla torma known as Shongpa Namdak had been offered in a skull cup, and this torma had spun around, turning to face the Karmapa. This close relationship with Mahākāla continued in the Karmapa's dreams and meditative experiences. A dark man, for example, gave him prophecies, and there were numerous other extraordinary signs like these.

The Karmapa kept two pet *hapa* dogs, a breed that is small and sprightly. After the first and then the second one died, they both remained in meditation as a great practitioner does, which astounded the people who witnessed it. When some mice were eating the offering tormas in the Karmapa's quarters, he said with great authority, "Do not eat the torma!" and the mice stopped.

During tantric feasts, the Karmapa usually did not take even a drop of the ritual offering of liquor, but one time he consumed three large jugs of alcohol all at once. Nevertheless, in his own experience it seemed as if he had not taken even a small cup. This reminded people of the life story of the great Indian master Virupa, who could consume vast amounts of alcohol without getting inebriated. In the spiritual biography of Khakhyap Dorjé, one can read at length about his incredible deeds, the wondrous signs, and how his realization allowed him to completely free his own mind and mature the minds of others.

Just before passing away, the Karmapa gave his Last Testament with a seal of secrecy to Gelong Jamtsül. Then at the age of fifty-two, during the twenty-second day of the third month in the year of the Water Dog from the fifteenth cycle of sixty years (1922), Khakhyap Dorjé demonstrated the manner of passing into the expanse of all phenomena.

His main disciples included the Eleventh Situ Pema Wangchok Gyalpo, the Second Jamgön Kongtrul Palden Khyentsé Öser (the Karmapa's son), the Eleventh Gyaltsap Drakpa Gyatso, and the Tenth Pawo Tsuklak Mawa.

1. The Sixteenth Karmapa Rangjung Rigpe Dorje
2. Tsepakmé
3. The Twelfth Tai Situ Pema Donyo Drupa
4. The Twelfth Goshir Gyaltsap Drakpa Mingyur Gocha
5. Gönpo Chakshipa

The Sixteenth Karmapa Rangjung Rigpe Dorje

1924–81

To the east of Eastern Tibet, in a part of Dergé known as Sengé Namzong in the district of Tokden Khok, Rigpe Dorje was born to his father, Athup Tsewang Phüntsok, and his mother, Kalsang Chödrön. It was 1929, the year of the Wood Male Rat in the fifteenth sixty-year cycle on the fifteenth day of the sixth month. At the time of his birth, miraculous signs appeared: everyone heard the sound of lyrical melodies in the air, white light filled the family's tent, and the water in their large vessels and offering bowls turned into milk.

When the child was around four or five, he did many unusual and wondrous things. For example, he would playfully toss an egg from the roof of his home, and it did not break when it hit the ground. He pulled together the sides of his porcelain cup filled with yogurt and closed off the top. Afterward, this cup was kept in the chest of the Athup family treasures and could be viewed.

The Eleventh Situ Rinpoché, Pema Wangchok Gyalpo, dreamt that the previous Karmapa was sitting in full lotus while his hands held a bell and vajra crossed in front of his chest. He was seated in the space above the roof of the Athups' house. Meanwhile, Khyentrul Rinpoché of Palpung looked closely at the Last Testament left by the previous Karmapa and made his decision. The thinking of both rinpochés was in agreement, so they recognized this young boy as the unmistaken reincarnation.

In 1930, at the age of nine, Situ Rinpoché gave him the traditional long-life empowerment, ritual cleansing, robes, and his Dharma name. He also offered the young reincarnation the lay precepts. In 1931, Khyentrul Rinpoché first offered the reincarnation a ritual cleansing and then the Black Crown and other precious items, thus opening wide the door to auspicious connections.

Afterward the young boy traveled to the Jokhang in Lhasa, where the hair-cutting ceremony was performed in the presence of the Thirteenth Dalai Lama. Though at this time the Karmapa was not wearing the Black Crown that liberates upon seeing, the Dalai Lama in his pure vision saw it vividly above Rigpe Dorje's head. The minister Trimönpa said that the supreme, precious incarnation did not take off his Black Crown. Following the ceremony, the Karmapa studied and reflected on the Dharma for four years with Bo Gangkar Rinpoché as his spiritual friend.

When he was thirteen, the Karmapa journeyed to Palpung Monastery, the seat of Situ Rinpoché, and spent time studying with him and reflecting on the tantras and the major texts of the Buddhist philosophical tradition. When the Karmapa was fifteen, on the sixth day of the first Tibetan month of miracles, he took novice vows from Situ Rinpoché, who performed the functions of both the abbot and ritual master. The ceremony took place in the presence of the Chökhor Tashi Gomang stupa, which enshrined the heart relic of the Eighth Situ Chökyi Jungné. Situ Rinpoché offered the Karmapa the name Palden Rangjung Rigpai Yeshe Lungtok Chokyi Nyima Trinley Donkun Drupai De (Glorious Naturally Arisen Wisdom of Awareness, Sun of the Dharma's Scripture and Realization, One Whose Activity Accomplishes All Benefits).

Situ Rinpoché also gave him the empowerments that mature, the commentaries that liberate, and the reading transmissions that support, for the major cycles of the

Dharma including the *Treasury of Kagyü Mantras*, the *Treasury of Oral Instruction*, and the *Glorious Kālacakra*.

In 1944 Rigpe Dorje traveled to Bhutan, and bestowed on its second king, Jigmé Wangchuk, numerous empowerments including those of Marpa, Milarepa, Gampopa, and Mahākāla, thus gladdening the king with the nectar of Dharma, developing his mind, and planting the seeds of liberation. Afterward the Karmapa returned to Tsurphu.

Rigpe Dorje received from Situ Rinpoché in 1945 the empowerments and reading transmissions for Jamgön Rinpoché's own writings, known as the *Treasury of Extensive Teachings*, and also for the cycle of empowerments *Knowing One Liberates All*. When he was twenty-three, Rigpe Dorje received full ordination from Situ Rinpoché on the fifteenth day of the first Tibetan month of miracles.

In 1947 Rigpe Dorje journeyed to Mount Kailash and then through Mustang on Nepal's northern border to Pokhara. From there he went to Lumbini, made extensive offerings, and then visited the three main stupas in Nepal—Boudhanath, Swayambunath, and Namo Buddha—as well as the caves of Asura and Yangleshö linked to Guru Rinpoché. The Karmapa inspired the practice of more than ten thousand people in Nepal through the Black Crown Ceremony, blessing them with his hand and in numerous other ways.

From Nepal he traveled to India, stopping at Varanasi, Bodh Gaya, and other pilgrimage sites, and then in 1948 he journeyed north to meet the king of Sikkim, Tashi Namgyal, in the capital Gangtok. Rigpe Dorje gave the nectar of the teachings to the king, his ministers, monks from several monasteries, and the people of Sikkim. From there, the Karmapa made his way to Rewalsar, also known as the famous Tso Pema and related to the life of Guru Rinpoché. It has many islets of grasses, which were seen to circle around the lake, giving the Karmapa a special welcome. On his way back north, Rigpe Dorje passed through Kunu, where he taught the Dharma, and finally he returned home to Tsurphu.

In the following year the Karmapa received many teachings from Jamgön Khyentsé Öser, including the empowerments, reading transmissions, and commentaries for his own *Treasury of Precious Termas*, as well as the mahāmudrā (the path of liberation) and the six yogas (the path of method).

At the age of thirty-one, the Karmapa traveled to China in 1955 along with the Fourteenth Dalai Lama and about two hundred important lamas and leaders from Tibet. A Chinese secretary requested an audience with Rigpe Dorje, and when he came into the room, he did not see the Karmapa sitting on his cushion but instead what appeared to be something struck by rays of light, so he left. Once outside he asked the Karmapa's attendant, "Where did the Karmapa go?"

"He's in the room," was the reply. When the secretary entered the space again, the Karmapa was there sitting on his cushion. Since there was no window that could have shed light in that particular spot, the secretary was filled with great faith.

In the next year, the king Tashi Namgyal and ministers of Sikkim came out to welcome the Karmapa and accompanied him to the main town of Gangtok. There, with the Himalayas as a backdrop, he again gave empowerments and Dharma teachings. Turning south, Rigpe Dorje journeyed to Vulture Peak, where the Prajñāpāramitā sutras were taught, then to Bodh Gaya, Varanasi, and the city of Bheta in southern India, the birthplace of Nāgārjuna. He traveled extensively, revisiting the three main stupas in Nepal and touring Ellora and Ajanta, the ancient Buddhist caves near Mumbai. He also returned to Darjeeling, a famous hill town just south of Sikkim. Throughout his voyage, the Karmapa gave the Dharma freely to the faithful.

In 1957, the Karmapa went to Gangtok and met with the Sikkimese king. Rumtek's ordained community, known as Samten Chöling, invited the Karmapa to visit, but he declined, saying, "Later I will come in a leisurely way," thus foretelling his return to his future seat in exile. Then, traveling over the Himalayas, Rigpe Dorje came back to his home in Tsurphu.

A huge change in the situation of Tibet was close at hand, and the Karmapa gave a prophecy of what would happen. He also performed many ceremonies to promote longevity and benefit others. In 1959, he escaped through Bhutan to India. From the time of the Ninth Karmapa to the twentieth-century Dharma king Tashi Namgyal, the Karmapa and the king of Sikkim had kept an excellent relationship; the king maintained his commitments and gave generous support to the Karmapa. With the full acquiescence of the Indian government, the Karmapa and his entire retinue were invited to Sikkim. Once he arrived, Rigpe Dorje opened wide the doors of Dharma. Through making appeals to the Indian government, the Karmapa served as a leader who worked to protect and implement support for Tibetan refugees.

In order to provide a basis for the teachings of Buddhism, the Karmapa began to build a new monastery in 1962 on the side of a mountain in Rumtek, Sikkim. Following his wishes, the ordained and lay Sangha, the administration, and the lay people all gladly took up this challenging work while the central government of India also lent its support. Toward the end of 1965, they had completed the Karmapa's monastery, Shedrup Chökhor Ling (The Park Where the Wheel of Dharma Is Turned for Study and Practice).

In the following year, Rigpe Dorje, his four heart sons—Shamar Rinpoche, Situ Rinpoche, Jamgon Rinpoche, and Gyaltsap Rinpoche—along with the ordained Sangha, set foot for the first time in their newly finished monastery, which served as the Karmapa's main seat in exile. The ordained Sangha was placed under the discipline of the Vinaya (the rules that govern ordained life), which was written down. Thrangu Rinpoche was appointed the abbot of this main seat, and Tenga Rinpoche was given the position of vajra master, overseeing all the rituals and ceremonies. For the ordained Sangha, the Karmapa put in place the three practices that are the foundation for taming body, speech, and mind through the genuine Dharma: sojong (ceremonies for the reparation and purification of vows), the rainy season retreat, and the ceremony to release the Sangha from the rules of this retreat. Following the tradition of transmitting practices through actually seeing and participating in them, Rigpe Dorje also initiated regular monthly ritual practices, the sādhana practice of yidam deities, and several longer periods of intensive practice (*drupchen*) accompanied by lama dancing.

The Karmapa also built Tashi Chöling, a new monastery that served as his main seat in Bhutan, along with other monasteries in Nepal and Ladakh. He traveled widely in Europe, the United States, and Southeast Asia, where he gave the genuine Dharma to hundreds of thousands of people without any prejudice regarding religious tradition, race, or status. Throughout the world, Rigpe Dorje founded more than three hundred Dharma centers to serve as a foundation for Buddhist teachings.

Mainly to the four supreme tulkus, and also to the ordained and lay Sangha and people in general, the Karmapa gave the empowerments, reading transmissions, and commentaries for major cycles of Dharma such as the *Treasury of Kagyü Mantras*. Like water flowing from one vessel to another, he gave oral instructions on mahāmudrā, the six yogas, and other practices to the lamas and tulkus.

The Karmapa revived the printing of scriptures and sponsored the publication of five hundred sets of the Kangyur, preserving the texts of Buddha's words in over one hundred volumes. He initiated the woodblock carving and printing of three major texts related to practice: the *Profound Inner Meaning* by the Third Karmapa, *The Two Books* (on Hevajra), and the *Supreme Continuum* by Maitreya. From within his own Kagyü tradition, he brought out study manuals, the major treatises, and commentaries related to the five kinds of higher learning: validity (or logic), the Madhyamaka, the Prajñāpāramitā Sutras, the Abhidharma, and the Vinaya. He also published the "three radiant lights" that illuminate the ultimate profound practice: the *Jewel Light of the General Meaning of Mantra*, the *Moonbeams of Mahāmudrā*, and the *Rays of the Sun Illuminating the Two Books*.

When he was showing some signs of illness, he went to the Khuyin Meras Hospital in Hong Kong. While staying there, he said that his next incarnation would be more knowledgeable than he and famous throughout the world. Later, at an American hospital in Zion, Illinois, he told his attendants how his next incarnation would be born in Tibet, and gave other indications. At this American hospital on November 5, 1981, when he was fifty-eight, the Karmapa demonstrated how the mind departs for the expanse of all phenomena.

After passing away, Rigpe Dorje remained in meditation for three days while rainbows gathered, the earth trembled, and other special signs appeared. His body was brought back to Sikkim via New York. During the cremation at his monastery in Rumtek, many amazing signs occurred. His heart, tongue, and eyes were left as precious relics, and his radiant image could be seen within a circle of light around the sun. Disciples who were present photographed this miraculous event.

His main students were Shamar Chokyi Lodro, Situ Pema Donyo, Jamgon Lodro Chokyi Senge, and Gyaltsap Drakpa Mingyur Gocha.

The Seventeenth Karmapa Ogyen Trinley Dorje

1985–

In the Land of Snow, within a district of Eastern Tibet known as Chamdo, there is a nomadic area called Bagor in the region of Lhathok where emerald-green grass covers the mountain slopes. It was here, on the morning of the twenty-sixth of June, 1985, that the Seventeenth Karmapa was born to his father, Döndrup Tashi, and his mother, Loga. While he was still in his mother's womb, many unusual signs occurred. Once, when she was returning home with a jug of milk, an adult sparrow hawk—a type of bird that rarely approaches humans—landed on a rope anchoring their tent. Sighting him, the mother made the traditional offering by flicking some milk with her fingers. Similarly, a cuckoo landed on the top of their tent and gave forth a melodious song. His mother dreamed that three cranes brought a bowl full of yogurt. Above it was a paper with beautiful golden letters. "This is the letter of recognition for your son," they said. "Until the right time has come, do not speak about it to others. Guru Rinpoché has sent us to you." It was a very clear dream.

One time Loga and her son Yeshé Rabsal went into the mountains to check on their livestock, and they discovered a cup filled with milk in the midst of a cluster of grass. Loga said, "Today we have found something quite wonderful. It's very auspicious." After making an offering, she and her son drank it. Marking the spot so they could find it later, they continued up the mountain. On their way back down, the cup was nowhere to be seen; only a few drops of milk remained on the tips of the grass. Such unusual events were not infrequent.

When the Karmapa was born, a cuckoo again perched on top of the tent and sang beautifully for a long time. Afterward, the people of the area heard the clear sound of a conch shell resonating a long time in the sky; soon after, they heard the music of low and high-sounding cymbals along with the reed horns known as gyaling.

Three days after he was born, the Karmapa said very clearly, "Ama!" (Mother!). From the time he was born until the age of four, when he started going to the local monastery, a globe of light would move around inside the tent. His mother and everyone else nearby saw the sphere, which would come suddenly out of nowhere and disappear the same way.

One day, his mother had churned milk into butter and went to offer the first part of it at the shrine, where there were images of the Sixteenth Karmapa and the previous Khamtrül Rinpoche. The young boy said, "If you're offering that butter to the Sixteenth Karmapa, you can give it to me. I'm his reincarnation." His mother replied, "You really shouldn't say such things." The Karmapa's sister gave him the name Apo Gaga (The One Who Makes Us Happy).

Sometimes the young boy would set up a stone seat and, sitting on it, take two stones to play as cymbals while he recited many times the Seven-Line Prayer to Guru Rinpoché composed by Chokgyur Lingpa. Other times he would say, "I'm building a monastery," and make up different kinds of music. Even though he was a young child, he enjoyed what was natural to a noble person.

Once, when he was playing with Mönlam, the youngest of his older sisters, he said, "Look! Father has fallen down."

"Don't speak about such bad omens," she reprimanded him.

"It's OK. Nothing bad has happened," he replied.

Later that day, when his father returned, he reported that his vehicle had slid off the road, but all he had to show for it was a small cut on his thumb. There were other occasions when the child showed that he possessed the higher modes of perception.

The recognition of the reincarnation happened in the following way. After the previous Karmapa Rigpe Dorje had passed away, the four main tulkus gathered at the main seat in Rumtek to search for the Karmapa's Last Testament, but they remained empty-handed. Later it occurred to Situ Rinpoche that previously in Kolkata (Calcutta), the Sixteenth Karmapa had given him a protective amulet wrapped in golden brocade, and Situ Rinpoche had worn it ever since. When the thought of this came vividly to mind, he opened the brocade to find the Last Testament.

In 1992 the four main tulkus met at the Karmapa's main seat in Rumtek to consider the Last Testament. After discussing everything, the four decided that Jamgon Lodro Chokyi Senge should go and search for the reincarnation; however, he suddenly passed away, which was a tremendous loss and a great obstacle for the lineage. Then, following the indications of the Last Testament, Situ Rinpoche and Gyaltsap Rinpoche each sent a representative to Tsurphu Monastery, where Drupön Dechen Rinpoche led a discussion that included the chant master and the discipline master along with the main administrative officials. A search party was sent to look for the reincarnation, and just as the Last Testament had predicted, they found the unmistaken one. When the Last Testament was given to the father to read, a photograph later showed him encircled in white light.

On June 14, 1992, the Karmapa along with his parents and extended family arrived at Tsurphu, where they were received in a grand fashion. Led by Drupön Dechen Rinpoche, all the officials, high and low, including the chant master, the discipline master, and the main administrative officials, as well as the ordained and lay Sangha, and huge crowds of people, all came out to welcome the Karmapa home. For the first time in this incarnation, the Karmapa set his lotus feet on the ground of his Tsurphu monastery.

Back in India, Situ Rinpoche and Gyaltsap Rinpoche traveled to Dharamsala, the location of the Tibetan government in exile, to meet with the Fourteenth Dalai Lama. They showed him the Last Testament and offered a report of what had happened. The Dalai Lama himself said that he had experienced something like that in a dream in which he saw the place where the Karmapa was born. It was a very pleasant area of meadowed mountains without trees where two rivers flowed. The Dalai Lama also heard the sound of the Karmapa's name. Since the Last Testament and the vision of the Dalai Lama were in perfect agreement, almost all of the faithful trusted the validity of the recognition.

On August 2, 1992 (the anniversary of the Buddha's first teaching), Situ Rinpoche and Gyaltsap Rinpoche offered the young incarnation the hair-cutting ceremony in the most sacred temple of Tibet, the Jokhang in Lhasa. He was given the name Pal Khyapdak Rangjung Ogyen Gyalwai Nyuku Drodul Trinley Dorjetsal Chogkley Nampar Gyalway De (Glorious Master Ogyen, the Emerging Victorious One, the One Whose Activity Tames Beings, the Vajra's Creative Play, Victorious in All Directions).

The Karmapa's enthronement took place at Tsurphu in the following month of September on the twenty-seventh day. Early in the morning, Situ Rinpoche and Gyaltsap Rinpoche, holding fragrant incense in their hands, entered the great shrine hall. Attending the ceremony were high government leaders, delegates from the various areas of government, and over two hundred representatives from Sera, Drepung, Ganden, and the monasteries of the main branches of the Kagyü tradition, as well as other major monastic institutions. From twenty-seven foreign countries arrived numerous lamas and lay people, and from all corners of Tibet came more than forty-nine thousand members of the ordained and lay Sangha. The upper and lower Dowo valleys, the home of Tsurphu, were filled with the bright colors of tents. In the presence of an ocean of the ordained and lay Sangha, as well as throngs of well-wishers and the faithful, Situ Rinpoche and Gyaltsap Rinpoche installed the Karmapa on the golden throne of Tsurphu, the Ornament of the World, and opened wide the doors to profound and vast auspiciousness.

Afterward the Karmapa began his studies with the chant master Umzé Thupten Sangpo. Two and a half years from the time he started to look at the texts, the Karmapa had completely memorized all the volumes of tantras that were practiced at his monastery. With Khenpo Loyak and Lama Nyima, he studied the *Lesser Path of Reasoning*; for spelling, he studied the *Lamp of Language*; for Sanskrit grammar, the text known in Tibetan as *Yangchen Drado.* He also learned to write poetry, which included memorizing synonyms and classic analogies. The Karmapa's understanding of these fields of knowledge arose without obstruction.

He also inspired people's faith and wonderment by recognizing many reincarnate lamas, among whom were the Fourth Jamgön Kongtrul, the Eleventh Nenang Pawo, the Seventh Dilyak Dapsang, and the Fifth Ripa Selché.

During the restoration of the upper temple at Tsurphu Monastery, the Karmapa left a very clear handprint in the surface a stone wall. And on February 2, 1996, when he was walking up the mountain behind the monastery, he took out from the ground many Dharma articles, such as large and small cymbals. A month later, on March 3, the Karmapa was again walking the pilgrimage route that curved along the mountain tops behind Tsurphu. When they came to a place called Damchen, he left a clear handprint on a rock that faced west. Noticing the impression, the head secretary Lodrö mentioned it to the Karmapa, who replied, "It's the radiance of Guru Rinpoché's smile." Continuing along the path, the Karmapa left another handprint in a rock close to the Snow Tortoise Spring. The retreat master Panam saw it, but the Karmapa asked him not to tell others. On the northeast side of the retreat house above Tsurphu, there was a large rock with an overhang. On its surface "*Karmapa khyenno*" naturally appeared in red letters, which can still be seen.

That year, on the fifth of March, the Karmapa said that there were important articles to be discovered by the retreat master Panam within the area of Damchen, so he climbed up to the high ridge along with nine monks. After they had looked very carefully, they found three hundred and forty-three old and very precious coins made of silver and copper. They unearthed a jade cup with a white metal stand and cover, and also two wooden cups in different styles.

In India, over the years, Situ Rinpoche and Gyaltsap Rinpoche had submitted to the government in Tibet requests for the Karmapa to travel so that he could receive empowerments, reading transmissions, and oral instructions that were unique to his own tradition. This permission was denied. Then, invoking the compassion of the government in Tibet, the two requested that they themselves be allowed to travel to their homeland of Tibet, and this was also refused. Finally, with no other means at hand, the Karmapa decided with tremendous courage that for the sake of the Dharma, he must leave his beloved parents and country. During the winter at the end of 1999, the Karmapa made his escape from Tibet, crossing into Nepal at the border of Mustang, continuing to Nyishang, and finally to India, arriving on January 5, 2000 in Dharamsala, Himachal Pradesh. Here he met with the Dalai Lama, who was extremely happy to see him, and they conversed for a long time.

The spectacular escape brought instant fame to the Karmapa. His image and story flew around the world, spreading across the screens of CNN and the BBC and onto the front pages of the *New York Times*, *Newsweek*, and many other foreign news outlets. The adventure of the Karmapa was told in detail, astonishing the world and bringing tremendous respect for the teenage leader and his brave escape.

Now at last the Karmapa could receive the Dharma teachings he had sought for so long. From the Fourteenth Dalai Lama he received the novice vows. Then from Situ Rinpoche and Gyaltsap Rinpoche the Karmapa received, as water flowing into water, the unique empowerments, reading transmissions, and oral traditions of his own lineage, including the *Five Great Treasuries* of Jamgön Kongtrul and the Golden Dharma of the Shangpa. Instruction was also offered to him by the great teachers of his lineage: his tutor Thrangu Rinpoche, the retreat master Bokar Rinpoche, the vajrācārya Tenga Rinpoche, the master Khenpo Tsultrim, and the tulku of Benchen, Sangyé Nyenpa Rinpoche.

They gave him teachings stemming from the manuals of the previous Karmapas and their heart sons, which explained the five great treatises, the three major texts related to practice (the *Profound Inner Meaning* by the Third Karmapa, *The Two Books* on Hevajra, and the *Supreme Continuum* by Maitreya), the texts on discipline and the Vinaya, and "the three radiant lights" that illuminate the ultimate the depths of practice (the *Jewel Light of the General Meaning of Mantra*, the *Moonbeams of Mahāmudrā*, and the *Rays of the Sun Illuminating the Two Books*). The Karmapa also received guidance on the traditional rituals, which are visually transmitted, and on the creation phase of meditation with its visualizations. The *One Hundred Thousand Songs* of Milarepa and the Buddha's words in the Kangyur formed a part of the Karmapa's curriculum as well. In this way he completed his extensive studies of the sutras and tantras.

In 2002, the Karmapa called a meeting at Vajra Vidya Institute and invited Jamgön Kongtrul Rinpoche, Gyaltsap Rinpoche, and important lamas and representatives from all the Kamtsang Kagyü monasteries in Nepal, Bhutan, and India. This was the first great assembly of the Kagyü lineage, known as the peerless protector of living beings. The purpose of this gathering was to ensure the development of the practice tradition and the visual transmission related to the thirteen tantras that Marpa Lotsāwa had brought back from India. All those present decided that each of the Kamtsang monasteries would specialize in one of the thirteen tantras that was given to them and engage every year in its intensive practice. The gathering also discussed how important it was for the monks in the monasteries and the monastic colleges to study the *Root Grammar in Thirty Verses*, *The Grammar*, the *Guide to Signs*, and spelling; they should also examine texts related to the stages of the path, such as the *Way of the Bodhisattva*, the *Ornament of Precious Liberation*, the *Seven Points of Mind Training*, and many other treatises.

The Karmapa also turned his attention to the yearly Kagyu Monlam. In 2004 he took over as the head of the Kagyu Monlam Chenmo's activities, acting as the chairperson of the main committee that oversees the event. He also set up many subcommittees to handle the various tasks related to the Monlam and appointed officers to hold different levels of responsibility. For the actual practices, the Karmapa took as a basis the Seventh Karmapa's *Twenty-Branch Mönlam* and then reorganized it. He added compositions and praises from Indian and Tibetan scholars; prayers from the four earlier and eight later Kagyü lineages, which are chanted in alteration; and long-life supplications to the great lamas who hold the teachings of the four major lineages of Dharma found in Tibet (Kagyü, Nyingma, Sakya, and Geluk). These texts are available in Tibetan and have also been translated into English, Chinese, Korean, Spanish, French, German, Polish, Russian, and numerous other languages, making available to many people the opportunity to connect with the Dharma and their own potential for liberation.

During the Mönlam, with the exception of empowerments and teachings, the Karmapa sits on a low throne with only one cushion. The novice and fully ordained monks sit in their own sections; following the tradition of the Vinaya, they are arranged in the order of their seniority in training. Knowing through his omniscient wisdom what would be in tune with future generations, the Karmapa has composed melodies that are pleasing, easy to hear, and inspiring. For example, Marpa Lotsāwa's "Auspiciousness Blazing in Glory" was set to the melody known as "Bringing Swift Blessings," and the short mandala offering was given "The Melody of What Arises Spontaneously." With these tunes moving through the rituals, there is no chance to feel drowsy, lethargic, or lazy; rather, the mind is truly delighted. With a feeling of everything going so well, the eight days of the Mönlam seem to pass in three or four.

While the ordained Sangha is participating in the Mönlam, they shave their heads, wear the three robes, and maintain the posture of the five points of samādhi while sitting. Between the sessions of chanting, the Karmapa gives Dharma talks, explains how to visualize during meditation, and gives advice on other important topics. He also performs the ceremony of reading the names of the living and the dead and makes aspiration prayers for them with the entire Sangha joining him.

During meals, the fully ordained Sangha closely follows the Vinaya rules for training in the partaking of food. For the eight days of the Mönlam, the three and a half thousand monks are not allowed, for example, to grow their hair. They must pass exams on how to wear the three robes and are not allowed to leave their rooms after eight in the evening. The discipline masters are always making the rounds, so the rules are strictly kept, and the Karmapa himself keeps careful watch.

On the last day of the Mönlam, all the fully ordained Sangha usually go on an alms round, and at seven that night the cultural performances start.

Tibetans, Westerners, Chinese, Indians, Koreans, and Buddhists from many other countries perform prayers and songs from their own cultures' traditions of Buddhism. The evening concludes with the butter lamp prayer and everyone holding a candle to illuminate the night. All those who attend—the ordained and the lay Sangha as well as other people—return home bathed in a feeling of joy and delight that the Mönlam has gone so well. With the Dalai Lama taking the lead, the great lamas have showered words of praise on the Karmapa who, despite his youth, has accomplished such great activity.

Every year in the tenth Tibetan month (around November), the monks from about ten monastic colleges gather at Tergar Monastery in Bodh Gaya for the Karmapa's Winter Dharma Session. For twenty days, they engage in debate based on the Seventh Karmapa's *Ocean of Literature on Logic* and the tutor Namgyal Drakpa's treatises on classifications of mind and classifications of evidence. For the remaining five days, they discuss topics related to three major texts of the Eighth Karmapa Mikyö Dorjé on the Madhyamaka, the Prajñāpāramitā, and Abhidharma. During most of the Winter Dharma Session, the Karmapa gives Dharma talks and in-depth training. Beforehand he is responsible for preparing the Winter Dharma Session, and he also sponsors the event.

In 2009, on the twenty-fifth day of the first Tibetan month, representatives of twenty-six Kagyü monasteries in Nepal, Bhutan, and India gathered at Vajra Vidya Institute. For five days they sat together and discussed issues related to protecting and maintaining the environment. The Karmapa led this meeting of Kagyü monasteries, Dharma centers, and affiliated individuals, giving extensive advice on topics related to the environment and how to preserve the precious world around them. On the last afternoon of the gathering, auspicious signs appeared—though it was winter, a light spring rain fell and a gentle breeze fluttered the prayer flags.

In sum, the Karmapa has been engaging in vast activity for the benefit of the teachings and living beings. He is staying temporarily near Dharamsala, India, at the Gyütö Ramoché Tantric University. From here the banner of scripture and reasoning flies in the wind, and the stream of true experience and realization flows forth like a surging river filled with summer rain. For those who have fallen into the darkness of ignorance, the Karmapa is like a jewel in space, the precious gem sending out its rays and enlightening everyone with a deep sense of well being and of the goodness present within them.

Part Three

The Patron, Author, and Artist of the Illustrated Lives

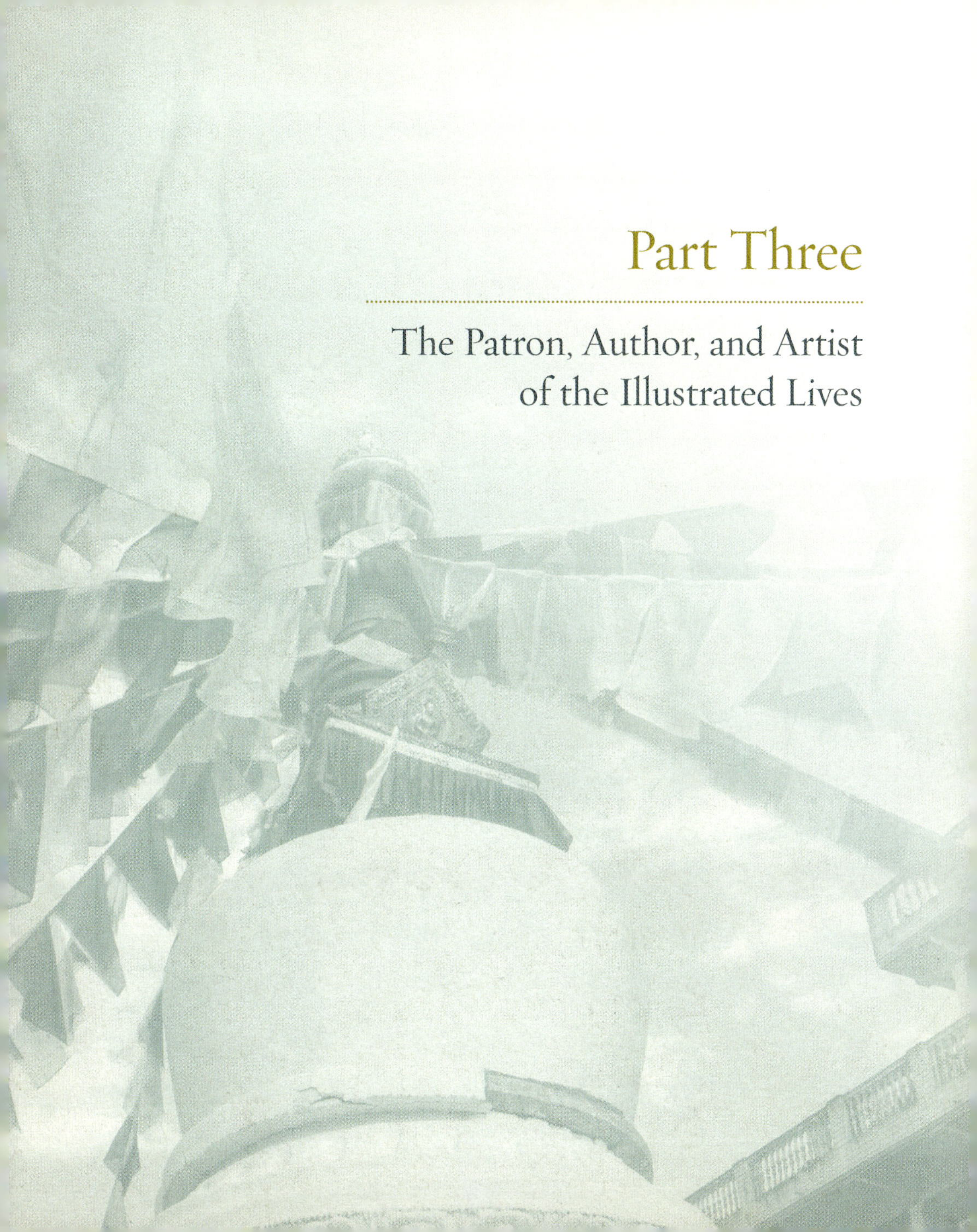

A Biography of Khenchen Thrangu Rinpoche

Khenchen Thrangu Rinpoche is one of the foremost teachers of the Kagyü lineage of Tibetan Buddhism. The senior scholar of the lineage, he was also given the degree of Geshé Rabjam, the highest scholastic degree, by the Dalai Lama. Thrangu Rinpoche is also an acknowledged master of mahāmudrā meditation, the most profound practice in the Kagyü lineage.

Rinpoche is the ninth reincarnation of the Thrangu Tulkus. The First Thrangu Rinpoche was recognized by the Seventh Karmapa as the emanation of Palgyi Sengé, one of the twenty-five disciples of Guru Rinpoché. The Karmapa established him in his own monastery, Pal Thrangu Tashi Chöling, located in the eastern region of Tibet known as Kham. Its monastic college for higher Buddhist studies became one of the great seats of learning in Tibet. The famous master Mipham Rinpoche stayed in a retreat house above the monastery for several years, and the great siddha Khenpo Gangshar gave teachings at Thrangu Tashi Chöling.

Amidst miraculous signs, the current Thrangu Tulku was born in Tibet in 1933 on the tenth day of the tenth Tibetan month. When he was still a young child, both the Gyalwang Karmapa and Tai Situ Rinpoche identified him as the Ninth Thrangu Tulku.

When the Chinese invaded, Thrangu Rinpoche escaped from Tibet, finally reaching Rumtek Monastery in Sikkim where the Sixteenth Karmapa had settled. The Karmapa appointed him Chief Abbot of Rumtek Monastery and the Nālandā Monastic College. Thrangu Rinpoche has been the teacher for the Karmapa's four heart sons (the regents of the Kagyü lineage) and for many of the Kagyü tulkus. In 2000, Thrangu Rinpoche was appointed one of the main tutors of the Seventeenth Karmapa Ogyen Trinley Dorje.

In the mid-seventies, Thrangu Rinpoche came to Nepal and built Thrangu Tashi Chöling Monastery near the great stupa of Boudhanath and Thrangu Tashi Yangtse Monastery near the famous stupa of Namo Buddha, which commemorates the Buddha's perfection of generosity in a previous life. Here, covering the top of a mountain ridge, Rinpoche has also established a monastic college, a school for young monks, and a great shrine hall for ritual practice. A medical clinic serves the monks and the local population with free clinics.

Under Rinpoche's guidance are several other monasteries in the northern areas of Nepal, including Manang, Nar, Nupri, and Tatopani. Rinpoche has also founded Thrangu Tara Abbey (a nunnery near Kathmandu), a school in Boudhanath for over six hundred children of the Himalayan region, and the Vajra Vidya Institute for Buddhist Studies in Sarnath, India, the site of the Buddha's first teaching. Rinpoche also rebuilt Thrangu Monastery in Tibet after the Cultural Revolution and then a second time after a devastating earthquake in 2010.

Thrangu Monastery Canada was completed and inaugurated in 2009. The resident lama, Lama Pema Tsewang, and his staff of monks come from Nepal. This large Tibetan-style monastery, the first in Canada, is Rinpoche's main seat in North

America. In Lumbini, Nepal, the birthplace of the Buddha, Rinpoche has built a branch of the Canadian monastery that represents Canada in the monastic section of the Sacred Garden.

Rinpoche has started many Buddhist Dharma centers, foundations, and places for long retreats in Europe and the United States, as well as numerous places in Southeast Asia, including Hong Kong, Taiwan, and Malaysia. For decades he has traveled to these centers, generously giving teaching, empowerments, and personal advice to his many disciples. He has also published numerous books in several languages, which emphasize teachings on the nature of the mind and on developing compassion. For his disciples and all who meet him, Rinpoche's kindness is as legendary as his radiant smile.

A Biography of Khenpo Sherap Phuntsok

In the mountainous region of Nepal's Nishang Drakar, Khenpo Sherap Phuntsok was born in 1981 to his father Sonam Dondrup and his mother Chozin Palmo. Of two brothers and two sisters, he is the youngest brother. From the age of eight, Khenpo Sherap studied reading Tibetan with his father. He spent many days of his younger years accompanying his father as he traveled to perform Buddhist rituals and recite long life prayers, taking care of their community. As a young boy Sherap Phuntsok was able to meet Kyabjé Thrangu Rinpoche when he came to Nishang Drakar. At that time, his father asked Thrangu Rinpoche to allow his son to become a monk at Thrangu Rinpoche's monastery, to which he gladly gave his permission.

In 1992 at the age of twelve, Sherap Phuntsok and his father took the long trip from Nishang to Boudhanath, where the young man became a monk at Thrangu Rinpoche's monastery. During the next four years, he studied how to play the various wind instruments, drums, and cymbals, and how to practice all the other aspects of the rituals for several tantric texts. He also memorized most of the texts recited at the monastery.

At the age of sixteen, he entered Thrangu Rinpoche's monastic college in Namo Buddha, Nepal, and for five years, he studied the five great treatises plus major texts from his own Kagyü tradition, the auxiliary topics, and other Buddhist writings. After finishing the shedra at the age of twenty-one, he was made an assistant teacher in 2001 by Kyabjé Thrangu Rinpoche, and began his teaching career.

During this time, he composed a summary of the essential meaning of the Middle Way based on Mikyö Dorjé's *Chariot of the Dakpo Kagyü Siddhas*. This profound text is famously difficult, and Khenpo Sherap's composition greatly pleased Thrangu Rinpoche, who wrote a foreword for the book. In 2003, at Thrangu Tashi Chöling Monastery, Thrangu Rinpoche awarded the title of Khenpo to Sherap Phuntsok, who was only twenty-three years old.

For the Kagyü Winter Debates in Bodh Gaya, Varanasi, and other places, Khenpo Sherap has almost always held, and still continues to hold, the responsibility for the classes on logic for students from Thrangu Rinpoche's monastic college. In 2005, the Seventeenth Karmapa Ogyen Trinley Dorje appointed Khenpo Sherap junior chant master for the Great Kagyu Monlam, and in 2012 he became the main chant master, a position he has kept until now.

In brief, from the year 2001 to the present, Khenpo Sherap Phuntsok has resided at Thrangu Vajra Vidya Shedra and at Namo Buddha, mainly teaching students the five great treatises. In addition, at the request of Kyabjé Thrangu Rinpoche, he has edited and arranged several practice texts in service to his teacher, such as the rituals of Kālacakra and Hevajra. He was also responsible for editing texts written by Thrangu Rinpoche, including his commentaries on *Entering the Middle Way*, the *Treasury of Abhidharma*, the *Way of the Bodhisattva*, and Dharmakīrti's *Drop of Reasoning* and *Ascertainment of Validity*, and also the fourth volume of the *Golden Garland of Kagyü Masters*.

A Biography of the Painter Lama Rigzin

From left to right: Khenchen Thrangu Rinpoche, Lama Rigzin, and Drupwang Sangyé Tenzin.

Lama Rigzin was born in 1970 in the Nangchen region of Eastern Tibet known as Salmo Gang. His village was Sipdatrong, located near the mountains of Sangri Barwa Tsegu. His father was named Daö, and his mother, Gapor.

Lama Rigzin had a brother who was a monk at Drupwang Sangyé Tenzin's monastery Dzapagön, not far from their home. When Lama Rigzin was about thirteen years old, his father went to this monastery and asked Palbar Tulku, well known for his clairvoyance, which of the two sons should study painting. Palbar Tulku replied that Rigzin was the one, so the young teenager started his study of painting, which would last eleven years. Lama Rigzin's teacher was the great master Sonam Nyima, the main painter at Dzapagön monastery. He was famous for the copies he had made of a series of thangkas depicting the Golden Garland of the Kagyü Masters, a set that was known as the Kagyü Sungenma and kept at Palpung Monastery. They are a famous example of the Karma Gardri, the style of the Karmapa's Encampment. Lama Rigzin studied these paintings in depth, and during the 1980s traveled extensively with his teacher to renovate many monasteries in Eastern Tibet. These included his main monastery of Dzapagön, Thrangu Monastery, Benchen Monastery, and many other Kagyü monasteries plus those belonging to other lineages as well.

In Tibet, Lama Rigzin had also come to know Tulku Lodro Nyima, the head of Khenchen Thrangu Rinpoche's monastery, and through this connection, Lama Rigzin met Thrangu Rinpoche when he came to Tibet in 1996. Knowing of Lama Rigzin's extensive training and exceptional talent, Thrangu Rinpoche asked him to come and paint the sixteen arhats in the shrine hall at his Vajra Vidya Institute in Sarnath. Lama Rigzin was happy to come as he also wished to travel to India. First, however, he went on a year's pilgrimage with his Dharma teacher from Tibet, Drupwang Sangyé Tenzin, serving him as an attendant. After this year of travel, Lama Rigzin entered the traditional three-year retreat under the guidance of Drupon Khenpo Laipu at Thrangu Rinpoche's retreat center in Nepal, situated near a cave of Milarepa.

Once this retreat was over, Lama Rigzin came to Thrangu Rinpoche's monastery called Thrangu Tashi Yangtse in Namo Buddha, Nepal. Here, on the walls of the main shrine hall, Lama Rigzin worked with a group of assistants to paint the images found in this book. After three years and one month of dedicated work, the paintings were completed in April of 2012 on the auspicious tenth day of the third Tibetan month.

Photo Gallery: The Artists at Work

Lama Rigzin

Khedrup Tenpa

Dondrup Sherpa

Dawa Tsering

Lama Rigzin refines the pencil drawing, the first stage of the murals.

Lama Rigzin mixes the paints of ground stone.

Dondrup Sherpa begins to shade in the colors.

The two nuns, Phuntsok Lhamo and Samten Chodron, add another color.

Three of the Nepali painters work on the later stages of Marpa's image.

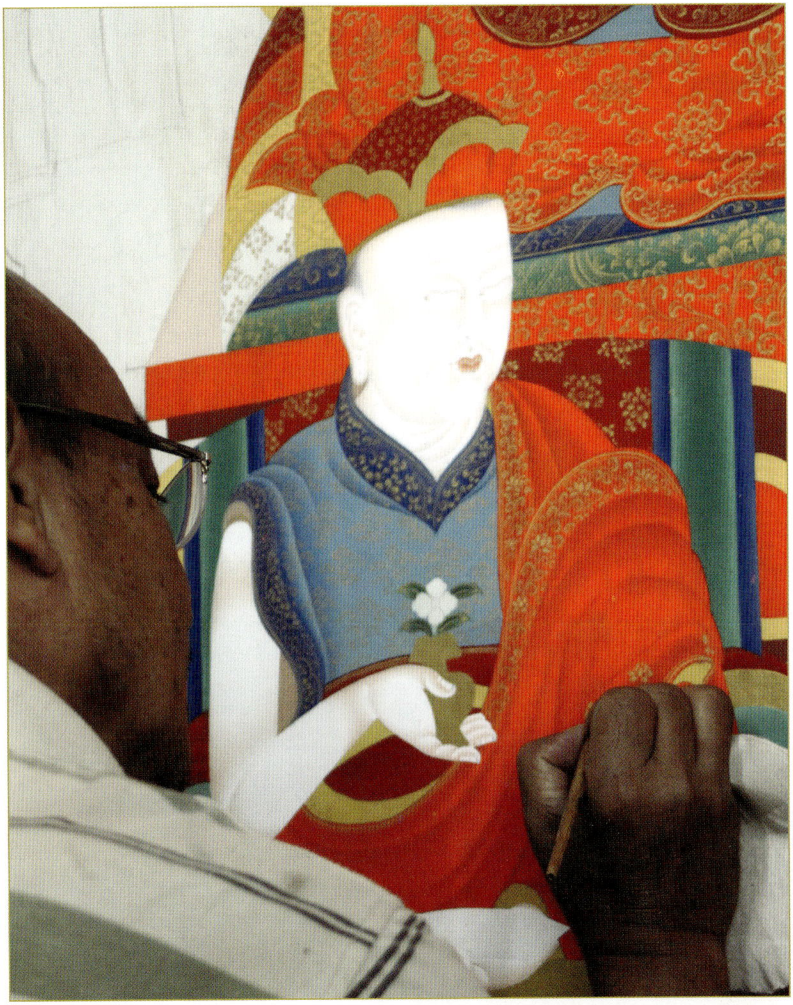

The gold overlay gives brilliant highlights that enliven the image.

Marpa Lotsāwa as painted by Lhadri Sonam Nyima, Lama Rigzin's teacher.

A Brief History of Namo Buddha and Thrangu Tashi Yangtse Monastery

BY KHENPO LOSAL

In Praise of the Buddha

ŌṂ SVĀSTI

Churning the ocean of the two miraculous accumulations
brings forth
The glorious perfection of the qualities that arise from
removing the negative and maturing the positive.
To you who reveal to the mind of every being all objects of knowledge,
Whether tainted or not, I bow in deep respect.

In Praise of Mañjuśrī

The radiant sun of speech, full of knowledge,
The light of your wisdom knows all there is to know.
You dispel the darkness from the sky of each disciple's mind.
Supreme deity, please bestow your limitless wisdom.

In Praise of Thrangu Rinpoche

As Vajradhara you embody the activities of all the Victorious Ones
While you manifest here in this realm as a spiritual friend, the glory
of your disciples.

Khenchen Thrangu Rinpoche flanked by Zuri Tulku and Lodro Nyima Rinpoche.

Lord of refuge, great scholar, supreme teacher, and genuine master,
Through all our lives you remain the object of our constant veneration.

Commitment to Compose
My mind cannot fathom just as they are
The qualities of this place of Dharma and pilgrimage,
And the way the eminent masters have blessed it,
But I will venture to say a few words while avoiding extremes.

After these traditional praises and commitment to compose comes a description of the special qualities of the stupa known as the Generous Offering of the Body to the Tigress. Famous throughout the world, it is one of the three major stupas in Nepal (along with Boudhanath and Swayambhunath) and the place where the Buddha in a previous lifetime brought to completion the perfection of generosity. This narrative is followed by a brief history of the glorious monastery, Thrangu Tashi Yangtse, which is built in this renowned place.

The Ancient Story of Namo Buddha

A long time in the past, many immeasurable eons ago, while the teacher, the perfect Buddha, was practicing on the path of learning, he was overcome with compassion when he saw a tigress tormented by starvation, and he offered his body to her without a moment's hesitation. The following story about this event comes from the *Jātaka Tales* of the Buddha's previous lives.

In the distant past there lived in this world a king named Great Charioteer (Shingta Chenpo), who ruled over a small kingdom of some five thousand subjects.

Due to the king's accumulation of merit, all his subjects enjoyed happiness and well-being. Rains came at the right time, while crops and livestock flourished. The king had three sons: the oldest was named Great Sound, the middle Great Deity, and the youngest Great Being. Powerful in the martial arts and radiating confidence, the two elder sons always helped the king in governing the kingdom. From his earliest years the youngest son, Great Being, was very bright and endowed with spontaneous kindness and compassion. He gave freely and generously to others as if to his only child.

One day when the weather was fine, the king along with his queen, sons, and ministers left the town for a relaxing time in the country. The king and queen rode upon an elephant while the sons, ministers, and retinue were mounted on beautiful horses. After half a day's ride, they arrived at a place of thickly wooded forests, resonant with birdsong, while nearby blossomed a tapestry of flowers in rich variety. The king was pleased with the scenery and ordered a large encampment to be prepared for everyone's enjoyment. The servants immediately unpacked everything, set up tents, and laid out a hearth of stones for cooking. Soon the ground was covered with tents as clouds billowed in the sky above. The servants bustled about, preparing a variety of foods and offering tea and liquor to everyone. Then the young people began to sing, dance, and play, transforming the encampment into a celestial realm. The king, queen, and ministers watched the entertainment while enjoying an eighteen-course meal accompanied by wine and liquor.

Then the three princes, in the full flush of their youth, picked up their bows and arrows and headed for the forest. As they walked along, they noticed a den in the dense woods. They crept up to it and saw inside a tigress sleeping beside her cubs. Great Sound and Great Deity laid arrows on their bows, making ready to kill the tigress, but Great Being stopped his brothers, saying that killing was completely wrong. When he looked into the cave again, Great Being noticed that the tigress was not able to move, for she had just given birth, and she also feared that if she left to hunt for food, another animal might harm her cubs. Tormented by hunger, she lay on the ground unable even to lift her head. Great Being was moved to tears with compassion that arose from the depths of his heart. He asked his brothers, "What kind of food would save the tigress and her cubs?" They responded, "This kind of red Indian tiger eats the warm flesh and blood of a recent kill. So if you want to help her and the cubs, you must find fresh meat."

Great Being thought for a moment: "It's indeed true that to save the tigress and her cubs, warm flesh and blood are needed. But then I'd have to kill another living being, and that would mean killing one to save another. What else could I do?" He thought for a long while, but did not find a solution. Then his brothers said, "We came out here to have a good time. It's pointless to worry about this tigress and her cubs. It's time to return to our parents." And so they left.

As he followed his brothers back to the encampment, Great Being thought, "For a long time I have been cycling in samsara, wasting countless lives, sometimes due to excessive desire, sometimes aversion, and sometimes ignorance. I have rarely met such an opportunity to accumulate merit. What real use is this body if not for the Dharma?" Finally he decided, "This time I must be truly generous."

Before he had gone very far with his brothers, he said to them, "Brothers, you two go on ahead. I have something to take care of and will catch up with you soon."

He took the path back to the tigress's den, quickening his pace. When he found the collapsed tigress, she was so exhausted that she could not even open her mouth. Great Being reached out his hand to touch her face, but she was so weakened she could not even bare her fangs. So the prince sharpened a splinter from a nearby tree and cut his body to draw blood, which he allowed the tigress to lick. Not long after, she opened her jaws and stood up. With a roar, she pounced on the prince and devoured him.

The two brothers waited a long time, but Great Being did not return, so they set out to find him. Reflecting on what he had said earlier, they had no doubt that he had returned to the tigress's den. When they arrived and looked inside, there was nothing left of their brother but blood, bones, nails, and bits of clothing. The tigress had consumed him. At this sight, Great Sound and Great Deity immediately lost consciousness; it was a long time before they recovered their senses.

The two then gathered up the pieces of their brother's clothing, and sobbing with deep sadness, set out for their parents' encampment.

During this time, the queen was taking a nap, and in a dream saw three doves flying high in the sky. As they fluttered around, a hawk struck and carried off the smallest one. Waking in terror, the queen immediately related her dream to the king. He replied, "Hearing your story, I believe the three doves are our three sons. The youngest of them, carried off by the hawk, is my most beloved son. I'm sure that something dreadful has happened to him." So saying, the king immediately sent out servants to look everywhere for his son.

Soon the two princes arrived, and the king asked, "Did something awful happen to my beloved son? Do you have any news?" Choked with sadness, the two were unable to speak or even breathe for a while. Finally they sighed deeply and told their parents that the tigress had consumed Great Being. Upon hearing this terrible news, the queen fainted away. The king too was overwhelmed with immense sadness and tormented by sorrow. After a long while and with profound sighs, the two princes, the king, and the queen rushed to the place where the youngest prince had died. When they arrived at the opening of the den, what met their eyes were the bones and rivulets of blood left behind by the tigress. The queen recoiled, overcome with sobbing, and did not recover for a long while.

Meanwhile, the prince had been reborn as Great Courage. He wondered, "What did I do to be reborn here in the celestial realm of Tuṣita?" With his divine eye, he thoroughly examined the five realms. Great Courage saw that gathered around the bone fragments he had left behind were his parents and two brothers. They were sunk in sorrow and completely miserable.

He thought, "My parents are experiencing such despair, it could threaten their very lives. To lighten their spirits, I'll go talk to them."

He descended from space to the lofty sky above them and spoke words of encouragement to comfort his parents: "I'm the prince Great Being. After giving my body in generosity to the starving tigress, I was reborn in the celestial realm of Tuṣita." With tears in their eyes, the king and queen said, "Son, you who are like our very heart, offering your body to the tigress was certainly most praiseworthy. But whom can we tell of our suffering in missing you?"

Great Courage replied, "Please do not be unhappy. The end of birth is to perish, and the end of gathering is to separate. No one can transcend this, for it is the nature of things. It is the same for everyone. If you perform evil actions, you will fall into the hell realms; if you perform virtuous actions, you will be reborn in the higher realms. Therefore, diligently pursue virtue. Make aspiration prayers, and in the next life we will definitely meet in a celestial realm." After a few more words, he disappeared.

The king and queen became a little happier and made the commitment to pursue virtuous activity. They created a small casket covered with seven kinds of jewels, in which they laid the bones of their son, and a stupa was built over the place in which it was buried.

The Namo Buddha Stupa dedicated to the Buddha as the prince Great Being.

The Region of Namo Buddha Past and Present

The pilgrimage site of Namo Buddha is about forty kilometers southeast from the Boudhanath stupa. Located on slightly elevated land, it is a pleasant and out-of-the-way place. The landscape below resembles an eight-petaled lotus, and the sky above has the form of a wheel with nine spokes. In this wide panorama, some mountains glisten white like a conch shell or a crystal. On other mountains, the groves of trees seem to gleam with emerald and turquoise jewels. In summertime, southern winds bring coolness; in wintertime, the warm, gentle sun is like the clear and radiant face of youth. The flowers bloom bright and multicolored. In the blue vault of the sky, clouds gently gather and turn all shades of red at daybreak. They are beautiful in wondrous hues that fill space with their canopies and banners. Like a heap of white silk scarves, mists drift slowly place to place. From the clouds, the drums of thunder resonate; lightning flashes like a slim dancer's quick motion; and fine showers fall in brightness. In sum, all the harmonious conditions needed to practice samādhi are present at this sacred site. Merely coming here inspires one's faith; renunciation and weariness with samsara naturally arise. As it is said, "In the supreme place of a solitary mountain retreat, any activity is virtuous." In brief, Namo Buddha is a place of pilgrimage highly esteemed by people from all over the world, east and west.

After Great Being offered his body in generosity to the tigress, people found it difficult to travel through the region for fear of wild animals, so they developed the practice of reciting "Namo Buddhaya" ("I take refuge in the Buddha") to dispel their anxiety. To this day, the local inhabitants call the area Namo Buddha. As time passed, villages gradually appeared, and cultivated fields extended from the houses. The ancient stupa has become a special place to accumulate merit through activities such as circumambulation and making offerings. People come from all corners of the world to visit the site

Ritual practice in the main shrine hall with the murals in the background.

and make the traditional offerings of butter lamps, a fresh coat of white paint for the stupa, and the pleated cloth that encircles the base of its spire and ripples in the wind.

In the past, when there were no roads for cars, only a modest footpath led to the site, and it was very difficult to reach. Nowadays, cars of any size can make the trip without a problem. In olden times, on most nights when the moon was full, a tiger would appear near the stupa; the caretaker and many local people would see it. It is said that later when cars, electricity, and other modern technology arrived, the tiger was no longer seen. Most of the local people in this area are Buddhist, and even to this day some can read Sanskrit.

About eight kilometers below the stupa, in the town of Panauti are ruins said to be the palace of the king Great Charioteer. Even today, on the fifteenth day of the fourth Tibetan month (the day of the Buddha's enlightenment and passing away), the people of the region have the custom of setting out a gilded bronze statue of the Buddha and gathering to perform ceremonies all day. At another interesting site about three kilometers below the stupa, a small temple is said to contain the remains of the prince Great Being's mother. Inside one can see an image of her carved into stone. Further, in the woods below the stupa, a little spring gives what is known as blessed water. About a fifteen-minute walk up from the stupa, one can visit the place where the prince offered his body in great generosity. Today, two caves are venerated, one near the monastery and another on a hill nearby. Since so many centuries have passed, the exact place is difficult to locate. It is certain, however, that the cave is in this locale.

Many great individuals have set foot in Namo Buddha. From India came scholars and meditation masters, such as the noble Vasubandhu and the unequaled Jowo Jé, the glorious Atiśa. From the Kagyü tradition, known as the protectors of beings, great lamas have visited, such as Situ Chökyi Jungné and his attendant the great scholar Bero Lotsāwa Tsewang Kunkhyap as well as the 16th Gyalwang Karmapa, Rigpe Dorje, the Drukchen Khyapgön Rinpoché, and the Drikung Khyapgön Rinpoché. From the early tradition of the Nyingma, important lamas have traveled here, such as Khyapjé Dudjom Rinpoche, Dilgo Khyentse Rinpoche, Drupwang Pema Norbu, Chatral Rinpoche, and Khenchen Jigme Phuntsok. From the glorious Sakyapa tradition, great individuals belonging to the Sakya, Ngorpa, and Tsawa schools have come, as well as major scholars and meditation masters from the Mount Ganden (Geluk) tradition, such as Khewang Gendun Chöphel. In sum, numerous important figures from all the traditions have walked this land.

Khenchen Thrangu Rinpoche on his throne in the main shrine hall, and on the high throne behind him, an image of H. H. the Dalai Lama and H. H. the Gyalwang Karmapa.

The Inspiration

Understanding how special this sacred place is and disregarding all hardship, Khyapje Thrangu Rinpoche worked long years to establish the monastery.

As there were no roads or water, the conditions were very basic at first. Not shying away from difficulties, Thrangu Rinpoche considered the teachings of the Buddha and in particular those of the Kagyü tradition. He set as a goal the establishment of three sections in the monastery: a monastic college focused on the study of Buddhist philosophy, a practice assembly focused on meditation, and a group focused on various aspects of work at the monastery. One purpose was to serve the entire world in pacifying all misfortune, such as sickness, famine, fighting, and quarrels. Another was to bring people onto the path of peace and nonviolence so that they might attain the temporary benefit of rebirth in the higher realms and the ultimate benefit of definitive liberation. This quotation illustrates how such a deep aspiration to benefit others manifests:

> Noble individuals do not announce what they plan to do.
> Since they do not make a promise easily,
> As if it were inscribed in stone,
> Their promise will not change even if they pass away.

When Thrangu Rinpoche was starting these three sections of Dharma activity at the monastery, since there was no motorable road, he had to walk the twelve kilometers from Dhulikhel many times. Also, in those days he had no personal quarters and electricity had not yet arrived. From all points of view, the conditions were very simple, and he had to make tremendous efforts. Without a doubt, the saying is true: "The Buddha does not tire of benefiting living beings."

A Description of the Monastic Complex

What follows is a brief description of Thrangu Tashi Yangtse Monastery and how its sections of study and practice are mapped onto this supreme pilgrimage site. The buildings follow the functions of a traditional Tibetan monastery with adjustments for the special elements of the site and Thrangu Rinpoche's deep interest in education and architecture. In the center is the main temple building,

The main shrine hall with the Himalayas in the background.

which is six stories high with another added by the curved golden roof in the Indian style. Counting from the ground up, the principal temple hall is located on the fourth floor. It has thirty-six pillars, each of which enshrines a gilded bronze Buddha at the top. In the front of the hall are statues of the seven generations of buddhas, which were created in Bangkok. In the middle is Śākyamuni, flanked by the buddhas of the past and future: Sarvavid Vairocana, Uṣṇīṣavijayā, Viśvabhū, Krakucchanda, Kanakamuni, and Kāśyapa Buddhas. Behind these seven, the thousand buddhas of the Fortunate Era fill the rows of alcoves. Fifteen mandalas from the great tantras adorn the ceiling. Hidden behind the main shrine is a special sanctuary, and outside in the front of the building is a wide veranda. These all represent the characteristics of a great temple hall as described in the Vinaya.

The three-story hidden sanctuary enshrines a central statue of the Victorious One (the Buddha of our times), flanked by the previous Buddha and the future Buddha. Here, too, rows of alcoves are filled with the thousand buddhas of the Fortunate Era. In front of them, turquoise dragons spiral up a set of pillars, so real they seem alive.

On the exterior of the building, starting from the highest point, a two-story curved roof in the Indian style rises in the center above the sanctuary. The upper roof is decorated with the beautiful symbols of the five buddha families: the Dharma wheel, vajra, jewel, lotus, and double vajra. Makaras (water dragons) with jewel horns extend from the four corners of the roof, which is encircled by garlands of gems and interlaced pendant jewels. The lower roof is graced with a small balcony and railing. On either side of this central roof rise two smaller roofs, ornamented with a gilded bronze finial. Below is a wide band of dark color, decorated with golden medallions depicting auspicious symbols.

In sum, it could be said:

> If one creates in earnest the armor of bodhicitta,
> It is like the treasury of space offering unlimited largesse.
> For fortunate beings, this temple and all it contains
> Are like the wondrous bursting forth of spring.

To the east of the main temple is a five-story building containing everything needed to feed the community: a kitchen, the steward's offices and storage rooms, dining rooms for the Sangha, and a reception room for benefactors. Beyond this is a small two-story building that houses an auxiliary kitchen and offices. To the southeast of the main temple is a modern, four-story medical clinic. Nearby is the terrace for lama-dancing, which has one side built into the hill and the other three supported by a single story of rooms. These are now the home of the Shree Mangal Dvip Branch School, which educates over a hundred young monks. These monks follow a progressive path of study beginning with the traditional sciences, which include the alphabet, grammar, and spelling. They then move on to read short treatises such as the *Thirty-Seven Practices of a Bodhisattva*. They also study ceremonies and the associated ritual tasks, such as making tormas (offering sculptures) and their butter ornaments. Mathematics and computers are also part of the curriculum as are English and Nepali. The school goes up to the ninth grade.

To the south of the main temple are several handsome, multistoried buildings, which are monks' quarters. To the west of the main temple are the eight traditional stupas, plus a stupa for Thrangu Rinpoche's mother. Nearby the stupas is a guesthouse administered by the main office of the monastery. Along the way back from the stupas is a stone statue of the Buddha, in front of whom kneel his first five disciples. Between them is placed a stone vase that commemorates the story of how the Buddha and his disciples miraculously came from India to Namo Buddha. Here was unearthed the vase containing the Buddha's bones, from the time he was called Great Being, and generously offered his body to the tigress.

To the northwest of the main temple is found the three-story building of Dharmakara Publications, painted white and graced by a balcony. It contains resources for writing and translating, among which are copies of the texts and teachings of earlier scholars and meditation masters, in addition to those of Khyapje Thrangu Rinpoche. The shelves also contain videos and tapes that have been published as books or are being prepared for publication.

Next door is the two-story protector temple, which holds images of the lineage lamas including Marpa Lotsāwa, the practice deities such as the glorious Cakrasaṃ-

The main shrine hall with the dining hall in front of it and the Himalayan foothills beyond.

vara, the Dharma protectors such as Mahākāla, and the deities of prosperity such as Jambhala. In isolation on its top floor, monks engage in the preliminary practices of one hundred thousand repetitions of prostrations, purification mantras, mandala offerings, and guru yoga. Nearby is a two-story building designed as the Pure Realm of Bliss (Sukhavati). The base has the form of a stupa in the shape of a fine house; above it, the golden curved roof following the Indian style is decorated in the four directions with makaras dangling tiny bells that tintinnabulate in the wind. In the darker maroon band around the top are medallions of the eight auspicious symbols and the seven royal articles. Off to the side is a stone pillar commemorating the donors and inside is a statue of Amitābha.

To the north of the main temple is a retreat center with twelve rooms and a temple. Construction of the monastery was begun in 1978, and from then until 2000, five three-year, three-month retreats were held there. Subsequently, a new retreat center named Thrangu Sekar Retreat Center was constructed near Bhaktapur, close to a place where Milarepa had practiced. The main practices of the three-year, three-month retreat involve the path of method (the six yogas of Naropa) and the path of liberation (mahāmudrā). The participants also accumulate mantras in meditating on Cakrasaṃvara and other deities, and they practice the guru yogas of Marpa, Milarepa, and other great masters in the lineage as well. But retreat is not just about counting up numbers. There are initiations that mature, commentaries that liberate, and reading transmissions that lend support, so the mantras are repeated in accord with these three to make them authentic. As Vasubandhu wrote:

> By listening and reflecting while maintaining discipline,
> You will perfectly connect with meditation.

To the northeast of the main temple are the structures that house the monastic college, including a smaller shrine hall and classrooms. Surrounding these buildings are inviting gardens where one finds many different flowers, jewel-shaped juniper bushes, and a variety of trees. Among all the treatises and sciences, the main ones for study and reflection are the manuals of the Karma Kagyü tradition. These include the Eighth Karmapa Mikyö Dorjé's extensive commentaries on major treatises, the great commentary on grammar by Situ Chökyi Jungné, and other texts on the traditional sciences. Over the course of the seven-year program, students investigate the five major texts, which cover logic and dialectics, Madhyamaka (the Middle Way philosophy), the Vinaya (monastic discipline), the Abhidharma (higher knowledge), and the Prajñāpāramitā sutras (Perfection of Wisdom Sutras), all of which are supplemented with studying other fields of knowledge.

When studies are completed, Khyapje Thrangu Rinpoche gives a certificate to the graduates. Then, in accord with each student's knowledge and the extent of his dedication, he is given a position: some become teaching assistants on the way to becoming khenpos (teaching abbots), a few become teachers in the school, and others enter retreat.

Residing in infinite pure realms, the buddhas and bodhisattvas
Utter auspicious words and cast flowers on this remote mountain retreat.
Holding a treasury of the three trainings, the community robed in saffron
Hastens to practice listening, reflecting, and meditation. How wondrous!

The qualities found in this majestic place
I have recounted honestly but only in part.
If any merit is due, may it plant the seed of liberation
In the mental ground of all living beings, our mothers.

This was completed on March 8, 2007 at the supreme pilgrimage site of Namo Buddha by Khenpo Losel. Michele Martin translated this in honor of the opening ceremony of Thrangu Tashi Yangtse at this sacred site in 2008.

Acknowledgments

Everything arises in dependence and this book is no exception. All along the way, many people have contributed with a generosity of spirit and an abundance of expertise. First, Raju Bandari took archival-quality photographs of the murals. With great patience Gen Nyima Tsering answered questions from his vast store of knowledge. Charles E. Manson gave valuable advice on the Karma Pakṣi chapter, while Christopher P. Atwood in particular, along with Vesna Wallace and Alex Berzin, added their invaluable knowledge about the Mongolian world and language. Ani Lodro Lhamo helped with Chinese spellings and customs. David Karma Choephel, Tracy Davis, and Steve Gilbert gave very useful comments on the manuscript. Lodro Rabgye created the cover and book design for the Nepali edition with help from David Karma Choephel, Rafael Ortet, and Keshar Joshi. Thanks as well to Karma Jangchup and Tashi Paljor for their excellent photos, and to Ling-Lung Chen for her support. A heartfelt gratitude goes out to everyone.

Glossary

Abhidharma. One of the sections of the three baskets or divisions of the teachings: the Vinaya, the Sutra, and the Abhidharma. It deals with the many classifications of terms that structure Buddhist analyses of the mind. Sometimes translated as "Buddhist phenomenology."

Avalokiteśvara (Skt.; Tib. *chenresik*). The embodiment of the compassion of all the Buddhas. His mantra is Oṃ Maṇi Padme Hūṃ.

bodhicitta (Skt.). The commitment to become enlightened for the sake of all living beings so that they, too, may attain the same state. There are two types: absolute bodhicitta is seeing directly into the nature of the mind, and relative bodhicitta constitutes the practices, such as generosity, which lead to this realization and which are motivated by the intention to benefit all living beings.

bodhisattva (Skt.). Someone who is committed to practicing the Dharma and reaching full awakening for the sake of all living beings.

cakravartin (Skt.). A universal monarch who, according to ancient Indian tradition, ruled multiple continents. Worldly people would consider this the highest human achievement.

dāka (Skt.). A male figure present in the retinue of major deities, and in some ways like the dākiṇī, though not appearing nearly as often.

dākiṇī (Skt.). This term has a range of meanings; it usually refers to a yoginī or an advanced female practitioner, to a female deity embodying wisdom, or to a consort.

damaru (Skt.). A small two-sided hand drum with strikers on either side, usually played with the right hand while the left plays a bell.

dharmakāya. See *kāyas*.

doha (Skt.). A spontaneous song manifesting spiritual realization.

eight auspicious symbols. (1) excellent umbrella, (2) paired gold fish, (3) treasure vase, (4) lotus, (5) white conch shell coiling to the right, (6) knot of eternity, (7) victory banner, and (8) wheel of the teachings.

eight worldly concerns. The preoccupations that keep us circling in samsara: gain and loss, fame and disgrace, praise and blame, pleasure and pain.

eight later Kagyü lineages. The founders of these eight were all important students of Phakmo Drupa (1110–70). (1) Drikung Kagyü, founded by Kyopa Jikten Sumgön; (2) Taklung Kagyü, founded by Thangpa Tashi Palwa; (3) Trophu Kagyü, founded by Gyaltsa Rinchen Gön and Kunden Repa; (4) Lingré Kagyü founded by Lingré Pema Dorjé; (5) Martsang Kagyü, founded by Chöjé Marpa Drupthop (not the same as Marpa Lotsāwa); (6) Yelpa Kagyü, founded by Yelpa Yeshé Tsekpa; (7) Yasang Kagyü, founded by Sarwa Yeshé Sengé; and (8) Shuksep Kagyü, founded by Nyiphu Gyergom Chenpo.

five Dharmas of Maitreya. Five major texts given by Maitreya to Asaṅga, who wrote them down, composed explanations of them, and taught them. They are studied in all the Tibetan traditions and refer to: *Mahāyānasūtra-alaṃkāra* (*Ornament of the Mahāyāna Sutras*); *Madhyānta-vibhāga* (*Distinguishing the Middle from Extremes*); *Dharmadharmatā-vibhāga* (*Distinguishing Phenomena from Their True*

Nature); *Ratnagotra-vibhāga*, more commonly known as the *Mahāyāna-anuttaratantra-śāstra* (the *Supreme Continuum*); and *Abhisamaya-alaṃkāra* (*Ornament of Realization*).

four earlier Kagyü lineages. Barom Kagyü, founded by Barom Rompa Darma Wangchuk; Phakdru Kagyü, founded by Phakmo Drupa Dorjé Gyalpo; Kamtsang Kagyü, founded by the First Karmapa Düsum Khyenpa; and Tsalpa Kagyü, founded by Shang Yudrakpa Tsödru Drakpa, also known as Lama Shang.

four great celebrations. The four major observances from the life of the Buddha: the day of his display of miracles; the day of his birth, enlightenment, and parinirvana; the day of his first turning the wheel of Dharma; and the day of his descent from the realm of Tuṣita, where he taught his mother.

four kāyas. See *kāyas*.

garuḍa (Skt.). A legendary bird able to soar deep into space, whose chicks spread their wings in flight from the moment they are born.

geshé. A spiritual friend. Often part of a teacher's name. Found often in the Kadampa tradition, in later centuries this also came to refer to masters in the Geluk tradition.

gyaling. A wind instrument that has a reed and sounds a bit like an oboe. It is played during pujas and ceremonies.

hair-cutting ceremony. The ritual performed for a young tulku that signifies his becoming a monk. The ceremony includes the cutting of a tuft of hair from his head and his receiving a new name and new robes.

Jang or *Jang Satham*. Refers to Lijiang, a kingdom in the far south of Eastern Tibet, where the 10th Karmapa visited.

Jinasāgara (Skt.; Tib. *Gyalwa Gyatso*). A form of Avalokiteśvara, the embodiment of compassion.

Jowo Śākyamuni. A statue of the Buddha at twelve years old, the central figure in the Jokhang, Tibet's most sacred temple. It was brought to Tibet during the reign of Songtsen Gampo in the seventh century.

Jowo Gandhola. A precious replica of the Mahābodhi Stupa in Bodh Gaya, said to have been sculpted by Ārya Nāgārjuna.

Kadampa. The Buddhist tradition stemming from Atiśa and emphasizing the development of compassion through mind training. Gampopa incorporated it into the Kagyü tradition.

Kagyü lineage. Also known as the Practice Lineage for its emphasis on meditation. It encompasses four earlier and eight later lineages (q.v.).

Kangyur. The collection of the words of the Buddha, usually in 108 volumes.

*kāya*s (Skt.). The bodies of a buddha. The first is the "body of qualities" (Skt. *dharmakāya*; Tib. *chöku*), which are the qualities of a buddha's wisdom, love, and power. It is also known as the Truth Body. As its essence is wisdom, only buddhas perceive it. Since others cannot perceive the dharmakāya, buddhas manifest two different kinds of form kāyas. The "enjoyment body" (Skt. *samboghakāya*; Tib. *longchöku*), is visible to only those beings on high bodhisattva levels who have pure perception. The "emanation body" (Skt. *nirmāṇakāya*; Tib. *tulku*) can be perceived by ordinary beings with impure perception. An example of a nirmāṇakāya would be Buddha Śākyamuni; an example of a sambhogakāya would be Avalokiteśvara. Sometimes the buddhas are said to have a fourth kāya, an "essence body" (Skt. *svabhāvika-*

kāya), which is described alternately as the union of the three kāyas or as their empty nature.

Madhyamaka or the Middle Way. Focusing on emptiness, it teaches the view that is free of all extremes, such as existence and nonexistence, and free of reference point. Studied by all the traditions of Tibetan Buddhism. *See also* Prāsaṅgika, Svātantrika, and Shentong.

mahāmudrā (Skt.). The "Great Seal," an Indian tradition of meditating directly on the nature of mind. In Tibet it became a major practice of the Kagyü tradition.

Mahāyāna (Skt.). The "great vehicle," which stresses the Buddha's teachings on compassion, emptiness, and Buddha nature.

Maitreya. The future buddha, now residing in the realm of Tuṣita.

Maitripa (1007–ca. 1085). The Indian master who taught mahāmudrā to Marpa Lotsāwa.

The Middle Way. See *Madhyamaka*.

modes of higher perception. Usually counted as six types of supernatural knowledge or sublime states of perception: performing miracles, divine sight, divine hearing, recollecting former lives, knowing others' minds, and, for great practitioners, knowing that the defilements are exhausted.

nirmāṇakāya. See *kāyas*.

path of liberation. A way of Vajrayāna practice that works with resting directly in the nature of mind.

path of method. A way of Vajrayāna practice that works with the creation and completion practices with attributes.

Prajñāpāramitā sūtras (Skt.). Words spoken by the Buddha that focus on the perfection of wisdom and compassion.

prāṇa (Skt.). The winds that move through channels in the subtle body.

Prāsaṅgika (Skt.). A philosophical school centered on the view of emptiness propounded by the Indian scholar Nāgārjuna. While not making any assertions of their own, followers of this Middle Way school use consequences to draw out the inconsistencies in another's view.

Pullahari (or *Puṣpahari*). The residence of Naropa in India.

Rangtong. Empty of itself. See also *view of intrinsic emptiness*.

sambhogakāya. See *kāyas*.

seven articles of royalty. The precious wheel, jewel, queen, minister, elephant, horse, and general.

Shentong. Empty of (what is) other (to it). See also *view of extrinsic emptiness.*

siddhi (Skt.). On the relative level, this refers to special attainments that come through practice, and on the ultimate level, to the realization of the nature of all phenomena.

sindhura (Skt.). A bright red pigment made from powdered lead and used in Vajrayāna ceremonies.

six syllables. Refers to the mantra of Avalokiteśvara (Chenresik): OṂ MAṆI PADME HŪṂ.

six yogas. Important yogic practices in the Kagyü lineage involving inner heat, illusory body, luminosity, dream yoga, transference of consciousness at death, and the intermediate state.

Svātantrika (Skt.). A school of the Middle Way, based in Nāgārjuna's view, whose followers make assertions and set up reasons on a mere relative level while engaging in debate or explaining emptiness.

Tengyur. Commentaries on the words of the Buddha by great Indian masters.

terma. Texts or objects that have been hidden (usually by Guru Rinpoché or his consort Yeshé Tsogyal) and are later discovered by masters destined to reveal them.

thangka. A scroll painting that is hung in shrine halls or above the shrines in the homes of practitioners.

Three Roots. The lama, the root or source of blessing; the yidam deity, the root of accomplishment; and the dākiṇīs and protectors, the root of activity.

torma. A sculpted offering made of barley flour and other substances, placed on a shrine and then offered outside. Tormas can be very elaborate and tall, or small and very simple.

Tripiṭaka (Skt.). The Three Baskets, referring to the Vinaya (the rules of discipline), the Sutras (the discourses of the Buddha), and the Abhidharma (the classifications of phenomena).

tulku. A reincarnate lama, who takes rebirth out of great compassion and penetrating wisdom.

uncommon preliminary practices (Tib. *ngöndro*). A fundamental practice of the Vajrayāna consisting of one hundred thousand repetitions each of prostrations with taking refuge and engendering bodhicitta, the long mantra of Vajrasattva, mandala offerings, and guru yoga recitations.

vidyādhara (Skt.). A Vajrayāna master adept at rituals and able to preside over an empowerment or other ritual practices.

view of extrinsic emptiness. A view belonging to the Middle Way and emphasizing the radiant nature of all phenomena. See also *shentong*.

view of intrinsic emptiness. A view belonging to the Middle Way and emphasizing the empty nature of all phenomena. See also *rangtong*.

Vinaya (Skt.). The tradition of discipline followed by the ordained Sangha.

Vulture Peak. Where the Buddha first taught the Mahāyāna during the second turning of the wheel of Dharma.

yidam deity. Peaceful or fierce, yidams are embodiments of various special qualities of the enlightened mind, represented as images for meditation practice.

List of Persons and Deities Featured in the Paintings

The names that identify the figures in each painting were derived from the sources consulted to compose the spiritual biographies in this book, which are mentioned in the preface. The identification of the Karmapas and the figures surrounding them are further based on matching up all the dates that could be found for a particular set of masters, teachers, and disciples within a single image.

When possible, the longer names for these figures have been chosen since they make it easier to recognize the yidams and lamas. These are listed in the first column. The names painted in the murals near the figures are usually shortened due to the limitations of space. In order to preserve these original names, they are given in the second column within parentheses and placed after the longer names if the two are different. When a Sanskrit name was available, it was added at the end.

Person/Deity	Tibetan Spelling in Wylie
Attendant	*nye gnas*
Attendant Kuntu Sangpo	*nye gnas kun tu bzang po* (nyené, *nye gnas*)
Attendant Namkha Ö	*nye gnas nam mkha' 'od* (nyené, *nye gnas*)
Attendant Rinchen Pal	*nye gnas rin chen dpal* (nyené, *nye gnas*)

Person/Deity	Tibetan Spelling in Wylie
Barompa Darma Wangchuk	*'ba' rom pa dar ma dbang phyug* (Barom Darma Wangchuk, *'ba' rom dar ma dbang phyug*)
Bodhisattva Dripa Namsel	*byang chub sems dpa' sgrib pa rnam sel* (Dripa Namsel, *sgrip pa rnam sel*), Bodhisattva Nivāraṇaviṣkambhin
Bramsé Kunrik	*bram ze kun rig*, also known as *bram ze skan rig*
Chenresik Chakshipa	*spyan ras gzigs phyag bzhi pa*, Caturbhuja Avalokiteśvara
Damchan Kyebu Chenpo	*dam can skyes bu chen po* (Damchan, *dam can*)
Ḍombhi Heruka	*ḍom bhi he ru ka*
Dorjé Namjom	*rdo rje rnam 'joms*, Vajravidāraṇa
Dorjé Phakmo	*rdo rje phag mo*, Vajravārāhī
Drölkar Yishin Khorlo	*sgrol dkar yid bzhin 'khor lo* (Drölkar, *sgrol dkar*), Sitātārā
Düsölma	*dud sol ma*, Dhūmavatī
Eighth Karmapa Mikyö Dorjé	*kar ma pa sku phreng brgyad pa mi bskyod rdo rje* (Mikyö Dorjé, *mi bskyod rdo rje*)
Eleventh Karmapa Yeshé Dorjé	*kar ma pa sku phreng bcu gcig pa ye shes rdo rje* (Yeshe Dorjé, *ye shes rdo rje*)
Fifth Karmapa Deshin Shekpa	*kar ma pa sku phreng lnga pa de bzhin gshegs pa* (Deshin Shekpa, *de bzhin gshegs pa*)

Person/Deity	Tibetan Spelling in Wylie
Fifth Situ Chökyi Gyaltsen	*si tu sku phreng lnga pa chos kyi rgyal mtshan* (Situ Chökyi Gyaltsen, *si tu chos kyi rgyal mtshan*)
Fifteenth Karmapa Khakhyap Dorjé	*kar ma pa sku phreng bcu lnga pa mkha khyap rdo rje* (Khyakhyap Dorjé, *mkha khyap rdo rje*)
First Karmapa Düsum Khyenpa	*kar ma pa sku phreng dang po dus gsum mkhyen pa* (Düsum Khyenpa, *dus gsum mkhyen pa*)
First Shamar Tokden Drakpa Sengé	*zhwa dmar sku phreng dang po rtogs ldan grags pa seng ge* (Drakpa Sengé, *grags pa seng ge*)
Five Indian Yogis	*rgya gar gyi dzo gi lnga* (Gyagar Mirik, *rgya gar mi rigs*)
Fourteenth Karmapa Thekchok Dorjé	*kar ma pa sku phreng bcu bzhi pa theg mchog rdo rje* (Thekchok Dorjé, *theg mchog rdo rje*)
Fourth Karmapa Rölpai Dorjé	*kar ma pa sku phreng bzhi pa rol pa'i rdo rje* (Rölpai Dorjé, *rol pa'i rdo rje*)
Fourth Pawo Tsuklak Kunsang	*dpa' bo sku phreng bzhi pa gtsug lag kun bzang* (Pawo, *dpa' bo*)
Fourth Shamar Chen Nga Chödrak	*zhwa dmar sku phreng bzhi pa spyan snga chos grags*, (Shamar Chen Nga Chödrak, zhwa dmar spyan snga chos grags) also known as Chökyi Drakpa Yeshé Pal, *chos kyi grags pa ye shes dpal*
Gomchung Sherap Jangchup	*sgom chung shes rab byang chub* (Gomchung, *sgom chung*)

Person/Deity	Tibetan Spelling in Wylie
Gompa Tsultrim Nyingpo	*sgom pa tshul khrims snying po* (Gomtsül, *sgom tshul*)
Gönpo Chakshipa	*mgon po phyag bzhi pa* (Chakshipa, *phyag bzhi pa*), Caturbhujanātha
Gönpo Shaljor	*mgon po zhal sbyor*
Gurgyi Gönpo	*gur gyi mgon po* (Gurgön, *gur mgon*), Pañjaranātha
Gyalwa Gyatso	*rgyal ba rgya mtsho* (Gyalgyam, *rgyal rgyam*), Jinasāgara
Gyalwa Gyatso Yabyum	*rgyal ba rgya mtsho yab yum* (Gyalgyam, *rgyal rgyam*), Jinasāgara with consort
Gyalwa Ritröpa Darma Gyaltsen	*rgyal ba ri khrod pa dar ma rgyal mtshan* (Darma Gyaltsen, *dar ma rgyal mtshan*)
Gyepa Dorjé and Dakmema	*dgyes pa rdo rje dang bdag med ma* (Gyedor Yabyum, *dgyes rdor yab yum*), Hevajra and Nairātmyā
Jampalyang	*'jam dpal dbyangs*, Mañjuśrī
Jeön Chöwang Tulku	*rje dbon chos dbang sprul sku* (Chöwang Tulku, *chos dbang sprul sku*)
Jeön Döndrup Tulku	*rje dbon don grub sprul sku* (Jeön Döndrup, *rje dbon don grub*)
Jetsun Khölpoga	*rje btsun khol po dga'*
Jinasāgara	*rgyal ba rgya mtso* (Gyalwa Gyatso)

Person/Deity	Tibetan Spelling in Wylie
Kagyü Trinlé Namgyal	*bka' brgyud phrin las rnam rgyal*
Kagyü Trinlé Shingta	*bka' brgyud phrin las shing rta*
Karma Düdul Gyalpo	*kar ma bdud 'dul rgyal po*
Karma Ngedön Tengyé	*kar ma nges don bstan rgyas* (Ngedön Tengyé, *nges don bstan rgyas*)
Khachöma	*mkha' spyod ma*, Khecari
Kharnak Dorjé Gyalpo	*mkhar nag rdo rje rgyal po* (Kharnak, *mkhar nag*)
Khenpo Chödrup Sengé	*mkhan po chos grup seng ge* (Chödrup Sengé, *chos grub seng ge*)
Khorlo Demchok and Dorjé Phakmo	*khor lo bde mchog dang rdo rje phags mo* (Depak Yabyum, *bde phag yab yum*), Cakrasaṃvara and Vajravārāhī
Khorwa Dongtruk	*'khor ba dong sprugs*
Khyentsé Shenphen Dorjé	*mkhyen brtse gzhan phan rdo rje (khyi ra mgon po rdo rje)*
Khyirawa Gönpo Dorjé	*khyi ra ba mgon po rdo rje* (Kyira Gonpo Dorje, *khyi ra mgon po rdo rje*)
Kyopa Jikten Sumgyi Gönpo	*skyo pa 'jig rten gsum gyi mgon po* (Kyopa, *skyo pa*)
Lama Berotsana	*bla ma be ro tsa na* (Ngulchu Bero, *dngul chu be ro*)

Person/Deity	Tibetan Spelling in Wylie
Lhola Yakpa Jangchup Ngödrup	*lho la yag pa byang chub dngos grub*
Lord Gampopa	*rje btsun sgam po pa* (Dakpo, *dwags po*)
Lord Milarepa	*rje btsun mi la ras pa*
Lord Naropa	*rje btsun nā ro pa*
Lord Telopa	*rje btsun tai lo pa* (Telopa, *te lo pa*)
Mahākāla Bernakchen	*ma hā kā la ber nag chen*
Mahāmāyā	Mahāmāyā
Marpa Lotsāwa	*mar pa lo tsā ba*
Metön Sönam Gyaltsen	*mes ston bsod nams rgyal mtsan* (Metön Chenpo, *mes ston chenpo*)
Ming Emperor Yongle and his ministers	*tai ming gong mo dang blon po rnams* (Taming Gyallön, *ta ming rgyal blon*)
Minister of the Khan	*hor gyi rgyal po'i blon po* (Lönpo, *blon po*)
Mongolian Möngke Khan and his Khatun	*hor rgyal po mong gor gan dang rgyal mo* (Horgyal, *hor rgyal*)
Ngok Chöku Dorjé	*rngog chos sku rdo rje*
Ninth Karmapa Wangchuk Dorjé	*kar ma pa sku phreng dgu pa dbang phyug rdo rje* (Wangchuk Dorjé, *dbang phyug rdo rje*)
Nyenré Gendunbum	*gnyan ras dgen 'dun 'bum*

Person/Deity	Tibetan Spelling in Wylie
Palchen Galo	*dpal chen rga lo* (Galo, *rga lo*)
Panchen Shakya Chokden	*paṇ chen shā kya mchog ldan* (Panchen Shakchok, *pan chen shā mchog*)
Phakmo Drupa Dorjé Gyalpo	*phag mo grub pa rdo rje rgyal po* (Phakdru, *phag gru*)
Rechungpa Dorjé Drakpa	*ras chung pa rdo rje grags pa* (Rechungpa, *ras chung pa*)
Rikden Khandro	*rigs ldan mkha' 'gro*
Rongtön Sheja Kunsik	*rong ston shes bya kun gzigs*
Śākyamuni Buddha	*Shā kya thu pa* (Thupwang, *thub dbang*)
Sangwadüpa	*gsang ba 'dus pa*, Guhyasamāja
Second Karmapa Karma Pakṣi	*kar ma pa sku phreng gnyis pa karma pakṣi* (Karma Pakṣi, *karma pakSi*)
Second Pawo Tsuklak Trengwa	*dpa' bo sku phreng gnyis pa gtsug lag phreng ba* (Pawo Tsuklak Trengwa, *dpa' bo gtsug lag phreng ba*)
Second Situ Tashi Namgyal	*si tu sku phreng gnyis pa bkra shis rnam rgyal* (Situ Tashi Namgyal, *si tu bkra shis rnam rgyal*)
Seventh Karmapa Chödrak Gyatso	*kar ma pa sku phreng bdun pa chos grags rgya mtsho* (Chödrak Gyatso, *chos grags rgya mtsho*)
Seventh Pawo Tsuklak Gawa	*dpa' bo sku phreng bdun pa gtsug lag dga' ba*, (Pawo Tsuklak Gawa, *dpa' bo gtsug lag dga' ba*)

Person/Deity	Tibetan Spelling in Wylie
Shönu Sangtsöl	*gzhon nu gsang 'tshol*
shrine master	*mchod dpon*
Sixteenth Karmapa Rigpe Dorje	*kar ma pa sku phreng bcu drug pa rig pa'i rdo rje* (Rigpe Dorje, *rig pa'i rdo rje*)
Sixth Karmapa Thongwa Dönden	*kar ma pa sku phreng drug pa mthong ba don ldan* (Thongwa Dönden, *mthong ba don ldan*)
Taklung Thangpa Tashipal	*stag lung thang pa bkra shis dpal* (Taklung Thangpa, *stag lung thang pa*)
Tashi Drak	*bkra shis grags* also known as Yakru Repa (*gyak ru ras pa*)
Tenth Karmapa Chöying Dorjé	*kar ma pa sku phreng bcu pa chos dbyings rdo rje* (Chöying Dorjé, *chos dbyings rdo rje*)
Terchen Chöjé Lingpa	*gter chen chos rje gling pa* (Chöjé Lingpa, *chos rje gling pa*)
Third Gyaltsap Drakpa Paljor	*rgyal tshab sku phreng gsum pa grags pa dpal 'byor* (Gyaltsap Drakpa Paljor, *rgyal tshab grags pa dpal 'byor*)
Third Karmapa Rangjung Dorjé	*kar ma pa sku phreng gsum pa rang byung rdo rje* (Rangjung Dorjé, *rang jung rdo rje*)
Third Pawo Tsuklak Gyatso	*dpa' bo sku phreng bsum pa gtsug lag rgya mtsho* (Pawo Tsuklak Gyatso, *dpa' bo gtsug lag rgya mtsho*)

Person/Deity	Tibetan Spelling in Wylie
Third Shamar Chöpal Yeshé	*zhwa dmar sku phreng gsum pa chos dpal ye shes* (Shamar Chöpal Yeshé, *zhwa dmar chos dpal ye shes*)
Third Treho Tenzin Dargyé	*tre ho sku phreng gsum pa bstan 'dzin dar rgyas* (Treho Tenzin Dargyé, *tre ho bstan 'dzin dar rgyas*)
Thirteenth Karmapa Düdul Dorjé	*kar ma pa sku phreng bcu gsum pa bdud 'dul rdo rje*, (Düdul Dorjé, *bdud 'dul rdo rje*)
Tokden Gönpo Gyaltsen	*rtogs ldan mgon po rgyal mtshan* (Tokden Göngyal, *rtogs ldan mgon rgyal*)
Treho Karma Guru Thuchen Tsal	*tre ho kar ma gu ru mthu chen rtsal* (Treho Karma Guru Thuchen, *tre ho kar ma gu ru mthu chen*)
Tsangpa Gyaré Yeshé Dorjé	*gtsang pa rgya ras ye shes rdo rje* (Tsangpa Gyaré, *gtsang pa rgya ras*)
Tsasum Drildrup	*rtsa gsum dril sgrub*
Tsepakmé	*tshe dpag med*, Amitāyus
Tsepakmé Tsa sum Drildrup	*tshe dpag med rtsa gsum dril sgrub*
Tseringma	*tshe ring ma*
Tsuktor Dukar	*gtsug tor gdugs dkar* (Dukar, *gdugs dkar*), Uṣṇīṣasitātapatrā
Tsurtön Wang Ngé	*mtshur ston dbang nge* (Tsurtön, *mtshur ston*)

Person/Deity	Tibetan Spelling in Wylie
Twelfth Goshir Gyaltsap Drakpa Mingyur Gocha	*rgyal tshab sku phreng bcu gnyis pa grags pa mi 'gyur go cha* (Drakpa Mingyur Gocha, *grags pa mi 'gyur go cha*)
Twelfth Karmapa Jangchup Dorjé	*kar ma pa sku phreng bcu gnyis pa byang chub rdo rje* (Jangchup Dorjé, *byang chub rdo rje*)
Twelfth Tai Situ Pema Donyo Drupa	*twa yi si tu sku phreng bcu gnyis pa pad ma don yod grub pa* (Pema Dönyö Drupa, *pad ma don yod grub pa*)
Yangchenma	*dbyang can ma*, Sarasvatī
Yongey Mingyur Dorjé	*yongs dge mi 'gyur rdo rje*
Yongzin Namgyal Drakpa	*yongs 'dzin rnam rgyal grags pa*
Yum Dakmema	*yum bdag med ma*

Bibliography

English

Atwood, Christopher P. *Encylopedia of Mongolia and the Mongol Empire*. (New York: Facts on File, Inc., 2004).

——— "Validation by Holiness or Sovereignty: Religious Toleration as Political Ideology in the Mongol World Empire of the Thirteenth Century." In *The International History Review*, xxiv 2 (June, 2014), pp. 237–56.

Chokgyur Lingpa. *Karmapa, The Sacred Prophecy*. (Wappingers Falls, NY: The Kagyü Thupten Choling Publications Committee, 1999).

Douglas, Nik, and Meryl White. *Karmapa: The Black Hat Lama of Tibet*. (London: Luzak and Co., 1976).

Dzogchen Ponlop Rinpoche. "Brief Histories of the Sixteen Karmapas." In Martin, Michele. *Music in the Sky: The Life, Art, and Teachings of the Seventeenth Karmapa Ogyen Trinley Dorje*. (Ithaca, NY: Snow Lion Publications, 2003), 277–93.

——— *The Lives of the Karmapas* (Tibetan and English). Edited by Martin Marvet. (Sidhbari, India: Altruism Press, 2003).

Finnegan, Diane. *Karmapa: 900 Years*. (Sidhbari, India: 2010 Karmapa 900 Organizing Committee, 2010).

Gyaltsen, Khenpo Könchog, trans. *The Great Kagyu Masters: The Golden Lineage Treasury*. (Ithaca, NY: Snow Lion Publications, 1990).

Jackson, David. *A History of Tibetan Painting*. (Vienna: Austrian Academy of Sciences, 1996).

——— *Patron and Painter: Situ Panchen and the Revival of the Encampment Style*. (New York: Rubin Museum of Art, 2009).

——— and Janis Jackson. *Tibetan Thangka Painting: Methods and Materials*. (London: Serindia, 1998).

——— and Rob Linrothe. *The Place of Provenance: Regional Styles in Tibetan Painting*. (Seattle: University of Washington, 2012).

Karma Thinley. *The History of the Sixteen Karmapas of Tibet*. (Boulder: Prajna Press, 1980. Reprinted. Boston: Shambhala Publications, 2001).

Martin, Michele. *Music in the Sky: The Life, Art, and Teachings of the Seventeenth Karmapa Ogyen Trinley Dorje*. (Ithaca, NY: Snow Lion, 2003).

Mengele, Irmgard. *Riding a Huge Wave of Karma: The Turbulent Life of the Tenth Karmapa*. (Kathmandu: Vajra Publications, 2012).

Tsering, Tashi. "Situ Penchen and His Painting Style." In JIATS, no. 7 (August 2013), pp 125–92.

Tibetan

Chen Nga Chöjé Sönam Lhundrup Daö Gyaltsen Pal Sangpo (*Spyan snga chos rje bsod nams lhun grub zla 'od rgyal mtshan dpal bzang po*). *Chos rje dpal ldan sgam po pa'i rnam par thar pa yid bzhin gyi nor bu rin po che kun khyab snyan pa'i ba dan thar pa rin po che'i rgyan*, vol. 1, 27–174. In *Dwags po bka' 'bum, Khams gsum chos kyi rgyal po dpal mnyam med sgam po pa'i gsungs 'bum yid bzhin nor bu*. 4 vols. (Tibet: *'Ba' rom bka' brgyud*, n.d.)

Chimé Rikzin, Khenpo (*Mkhan po 'Chi med rig dzin*). *Nang bstan lha bris kyi lo rgyus*. In *Rgyal ba'i sku brnyan legs par blta ba'i sgron me*. (Taiwan, Choszhin Parkhang (Fa Ru Chubanshe), 2000), 6–23.

Mendong Tsampa Karma Ngedön Tengyé (*Sman sdong mtshams pa Kar ma nges don bstan rgyas*). *Chos rje kar ma pa sku phreng rim byon gyi rnam thar mdor bsdus dpag bsam khri shing*. (Life stories of the First to the Fourteenth Karmapas), 1–235. Khenchen Thrangu Rinpoche (*Mkhan chen Khra 'gu rin po che*). *Kar ma pa sku phreng gi rnam thar*. (Life Stories of the Fifteenth and Sixteenth Karmapas), 237–386.

Mikyö Dorjé, the Eighth Karmapa. *Kam tshang chos 'byung, Zhwa dmar cod pan 'dzin pa na rim la bsdus pa'i tshul gyis gsol ba 'debs*. 207ff. (Rumtek, Sikkim: n.p., n.d.).

Pawo Tsuklak Trengwa (*Dpa' bo tsug lag phreng ba*). *Chos 'byung mkhas pa'i dga ston*. (Sarnath, India: Vajra Vidya Library, 2003).

——— *Rje btsun mar pa'i rnam thar grub pa'i ngo mtshar brjod pa*. (Sarnath, India: Vajra Vidya Library, 2010).

Shamar Khachö Wangpo (*Zhwa dmar Mkha' spyod dbang po*). *Brgyud pa'i khungs nyer bar gleng pa*, 1–8. (Gangtok, Sikkim: Gonpo Tseten, Palace Monastery, 1978). TBRC #23928.

——— *Dpal prajna bha dra'i rnam par thar pa'i 'od mtsho'i zla ris* (Telopa), 8–99. (Gangtok, Sikkim: Gonpo Tseten, Palace Monastery, 1978). TBRC #23928.

——— *Dpal jnana siddhi'i rnam par thar pa grub pa'i rna rgyan* (Naropa), 101–85. (Gangtok, Sikkim: Gonpo Tseten, Palace Monastery, 1978). TBRC #23928.

——— *Zhwa dmar mkha' spyod dbang po gsungs 'bum*, vol 1. 4 vols. (Gangtok, Sikkim: Gonpo Tseten, Palace Monastery, 1978). TBRC #23928.

Shanak Dzöpa Tenzin Namgyal (*Zhwa nag mdzod pa Bstan 'dzin rnam rgyal*). *Dus gsum rgyal ba thams cad kyi phrin las*. (Sidhbari, Dharamsala, India, 2001).

Sherap Phuntsok, Khenpo (*Mkhanpo Shes rab phun tshogs*). *Dbu ma dwags rgyud grup shing gi spyi don dpal kar ma pa'i dgongs pa mdzes par byed pa'i rgyan zhes bya ba bzhugs so.* (Sarnath, India: Vajra Vidya Institute Library, 2003).

——— *Dbu ma gzhan stong la 'jug pa'i sgo gong ma'i gsung gi bdud rtsi bya ba bzhungs so.* (Sarnath, India: Vajra Vidya Institute Library, 2007).

——— *Rgyal ba'i dbang po sangs rgyas kar ma pa sku phreng rim byon gyi mdzad rnam snying po bsdus pa dad pa'i sa bon.* (Sarnath, India: Vajra Vidya Library, 2011).

Situ Chökyi Jung Ngé (*Si tu chos kyi 'byung gnas*). *Sgrub brgyud kar ma kam tshang gi brgyud pa rin po che'i rnam thar nor bu zla ba chu shel gyi phreng ba.* vols. 1 and 2. (Sarnath, India: Vajra Vidya Library, 2005).

Tsangnyön Heruka (*Gtsang smyon he ru ka*). *Rnal 'byor dbang phyug dam pa rje btsun mi la ras pa'i rnam thar rgyas par phye ba'i mgur 'bum.* (Taipei: Corporate Body of the Buddha Educational Foundation, 2003).

Index

C

K

N

U

Z

About the Translator

Michele Martin has been a Buddhist practitioner for over forty years and has spent the last thirty of those based in Nepal and India studying with Tibetan lamas and working as a translator of oral and written Tibetan. With two graduate degrees from Yale, she also had a long career in publishing and is a founding board member of the Tibetan Buddhist Research Center. Among numerous translations from Tibetan texts on philosophy, meditation, and history, her books include *Music in the Sky: The Life, Art, and Teachings of the Seventeenth Karmapa Ogyen Trinley Dorje* (author and translator) and *Gaining Certainty in the View* (translator). In cooperation with others, she has edited and translated *Song for the King: Saraha on Mahamudra Meditation*; *The First Karmapa: The Life and Teachings of Dusum Khyenpa*; and *Traveling the Path of Compassion: A Commentary on the Thirty-Seven Practices of a Bodhisattva.*

Also Available from Wisdom Publications

Essentials of Mahamudra
Looking Directly at the Mind
Khenchen Thrangu Rinpoche

"Makes the practice of mahamudra, one of the most advanced forms of meditation, easily accessible to Westerners' everyday lives. A wonderful way of bringing us to the path."—*Mandala*

The Mind of Mahamudra
Advice from the Kagyü Masters
Translated and Introduced by Peter Alan Roberts

"Quite simply, the best anthology of Tibetan Mahāmudrā texts yet to appear."
—Roger R. Jackson, Carleton College, author of *Tantric Treasures*

A Song for the King
Saraha on Mahamudra Meditation
Khenchen Thrangu Rinpoche
Edited by Michele Martin

"A lively commentary [on] a poetic classic of Buddhist literature. Editor Michele Martin has supplemented Thrangu Rinpoche's lucid commentary with notes and appendices that make the book as accessible for novices as it is rewarding for experienced practitioners and scholars."—*Buddhadharma*

Mahamudra
The Moonlight—Quintessence of Mind and Meditation
Dakpo Tashi Namgyal
Translated and annotated by Lobsang P. Lhalungpa
Foreword by His Holiness the Dalai Lama

"Has helped numerous serious Dharma students. It is excellent that the second edition is now being brought out."—His Holiness the Dalai Lama

Mahāmudrā and Related Instructions
Core Teachings of the Kagyü Schools
Translated by Peter Alan Roberts

"This collection is a treasury of 'great seal' teachings from the most renowned gurus of the Mahāmudrā lineage, each text precious beyond compare. Every page exudes freshness of realization, holding the keys to our own personal awakening."—Judith Simmer-Brown, Naropa University, author of *Dakini's Warm Breath*

About Wisdom Publications

Wisdom Publications is the leading publisher of classic and contemporary Buddhist books and practical works on mindfulness. To learn more about us or to explore our other books, please visit our website at wisdompubs.org or contact us at the address below.

Wisdom Publications
199 Elm Street
Somerville, MA 02144 USA

We are a 501(c)(3) organization, and donations in support of our mission are tax deductible.

Wisdom Publications is affiliated with the Foundation for the Preservation of the Mahayana Tradition (FPMT).

The Second Karmapa Karma Pakṣi

Mahākāla Bernakchen and Gönpo Shaljor